Carl von Clausewitz's
On War

A Biography

Other titles in the *Books that Shook the World* series by Manjul Publishing House:

Available now:

The Bible by Karen Armstrong

Plato's *Republic* by Simon Blackburn

Darwin's *Origin of Species* by Janet Browne

Thomas Paine's *Rights of Man* by Christopher Hitchens

Marx's *Das Kapital* by Francis Wheen

Forthcoming:

Homer's *The Iliad and The Odyssey* by Alberto Manguel

On The Wealth of Nations by P. J. O'Rourke

Machiavelli's *The Prince* by Philip Bobbitt

Carl von Clausewitz's ON WAR

A BIOGRAPHY

HEW STRACHAN

MANJUL
Manjul Publishing House

First published in India by

Manjul Publishing House Pvt. Ltd.

Registered Office:
10 Nishat Colony, Bhopal 462 003 - India
Corporate Office:
2nd Floor, Usha Preet Complex,
42 Malviya Nagar, Bhopal 462 003 - India
E-mail: manjul@manjulindia.com Website: www.manjulindia.com

Distribution Office:
SV Book Supply Company Pvt. Ltd.
7/32, Ground Floor, Ansari Road, Daryaganj, New Delhi 110 002
Email: booksupplyco@gmail.com

Carl von Clausewitz's On War - A Biography,
first published in paperback in the UK in 2008 by Atlantic Books,
an imprint of Grove Atlantic Ltd.

This edition first published in 2011

ISBN 978-81-8322-138-2

Printed & bound in India by Thomson Press Ltd. (India)

CONTENTS

ACKNOWLEDGEMENTS

I was invited to write this book at the end of 2003, when I had just returned from giving a series of lectures and seminars on Clausewitz at the Royal Norwegian Air Force Academy in Trondheim. Not for the first time, the fertility of Clausewitz's thinking had left my mind buzzing with ideas and I accepted the offer with alacrity. My first debt, therefore, is to those responsible for entertaining me in Norway, and especially to Nils Naastad, Ole-Jørgen Maao and above all Harald Hoiback, who made several suggestions for the book's improvement. Since then I have acquired an obligation to Andreas Herberg-Rothe. In March 2005 he and I organized a conference on Clausewitz in the twenty-first century, under the auspices of the Oxford Leverhulme Programme on the Changing Character of War, whose director I am. I should take this opportunity to record my thanks to the Trustees of the Leverhulme Foundation for their extraordinarily generous support of the study of war at Oxford. Hamish Scott, a friend of long standing, became a neighbour as I was writing: his book, *The Birth of a Great Power System*

1740–1815, was my *vade mecum* through Clausewitz's Europe.

Writing this book has cost my family another summer holiday, and I thank my wife Pamela from the bottom of my heart; she has even read and commented on this one. My brother Gavin Strachan has relieved me of obligations, both filial and rural.

A NOTE ON TRANSLATIONS AND EDITIONS

On War, or *Vom Kriege*, was first published in three volumes by Ferdinand Dümmler in Berlin between 1832 and 1834. It then appeared in a second edition with some alterations to the text as well as minor corrections in 1853–7. A third edition followed in 1867–9. Most translations, including the first English translation of 1873, by J. J. Graham, revised by F. N. Maude in 1908 (Kegan Paul, Trench, Trubner & Co.), were derived from the second edition, not the first.

In 1952 Werner Hahlweg restored the original text of the first edition, in what was by then the sixteenth edition (Bonn, Dümmler). This is the German version I have used. Hahlweg provides a full scholarly apparatus (unlike any of the English editions), and his text is now in its nineteenth edition.

In 1976 Michael Howard and Peter Paret published a new English translation based on the first German edition. As this is the version which is now standard in the English-speaking world, quotations from *On War* in what follows are – unless otherwise specified – derived from it (although their spelling is anglicized where appropriate) and page references are to the first edition, published by Princeton University Press.

In the process of comparing the German text with the English translations, I have found myself diverging from some of the interpretations embraced by Michael Howard and Peter Paret. Readers will therefore also find references to the two earlier English-language translations, even if they are not based on the first German edition. J. J. Graham's translation of 1873 was dominant until 1976, especially in the version abridged by Anatol Rapoport and published by Penguin in 1968. Both Graham's translation and the shorter Penguin edition are in print at the time of writing. So, too, after a long interval, is the version most faithful to the original German, that of O. J. Matthijs Jolles, first published by Random House in New York in 1943. I have used the edition published by the *Infantry Journal* in Washington in 1950.

There is no standard system of referencing Clausewitz, and the different editions in many languages result in pagination which is anything but uniform. Joachim Niemeyer produced a concordance to the German editions of *On War* in his edition of Clausewitz's *Historische Briefe über die grossen Kriegereignisse im Oktober 1806* (Bonn, Dümmler, 1977). Some chapters of *On War* cover several pages, and simply giving book and chapter numbers (which are consistent across all editions) is insufficient aid to the scholar. I have therefore adopted a reference system that gives three numbers. The first is the number of the book, the second is the number of the chapter, and the third is the number of the page of the edition from which I am quoting. If the edition is not specified, then the reference is to the Howard and Paret version in its original edition, as published by Princeton University Press in 1976. Where I have been unhappy with their translation and used another, or have referred to the German because I have found no other English translation wholly satisfactory, I have made that clear.

INTRODUCTION

In 1975, six years after returning from his last tour of duty in Vietnam, Colonel (as he was then) Colin Powell went to the US National War College. A year later, Princeton University Press brought out a fresh English-language edition of Carl von Clausewitz's *Vom Kriege*, or *On War*, first published posthumously in German in three volumes between 1832 and 1834. Two of the most distinguished historians of their generation, Michael Howard and Peter Paret, were responsible for the translation. Howard had fought with distinction in the Second World War: Clausewitz appealed to him as a soldier writing for other soldiers. His aim was an English version that soldiers themselves would read, and, just in case they did not, Bernard Brodie, a star of the strategic studies firmament of the nuclear age, concluded the volume with a short summary of the text. The Princeton edition of *On War* has proved far more successful than the German original ever was. It not only rendered Clausewitz's prose in language that is readable and graphic (as is the original), but also gave the text an inner unity which many of its readers had denied it possessed.

Over the last thirty years American soldiers in particular have responded to Howard's hopes.

One of them was Colonel Powell. He described *On War* as 'a beam of light from the past, still illuminating present-day military quandaries'. Confused by the disintegration in Vietnam of the army he loved, and alarmed by the gulf that had opened between it and the society it served, he found explanations for what had gone wrong in *On War*. 'Clausewitz's greatest lesson for my profession was that the soldier, for all his patriotism, valor, and skill, forms just one leg in a triad. Without all three legs engaged, the military, the government, and the people, the enterprise cannot stand.'[1] Powell was not alone in using Clausewitz to explain what had gone wrong in Vietnam. In 1981 Colonel Harry Summers, Jr, prepared a study for the US Army War College entitled *On Strategy: A critical analysis of the Vietnam war*. Published in 1982, it had already been printed three times by 1983. Summers applied *On War* (as translated by Howard and Paret) to identify the 'missing link' in US strategy – 'the failure to address the question of "how" to use military means to achieve a political end'. Summers, like Powell, highlighted Clausewitz's 'trinity', which he, also like Powell, maintained was made up of army, government and people. Feeling, too, that he had to justify his use of a text that had been published 150 years before, Summers insisted 'that this is the most *modern* source available'.[2]

Summers had no cause to be so defensive. In 1983 Powell became the senior military assistant to Caspar

Weinberger, the Secretary of Defense in Ronald Reagan's administration. Like Powell, Weinberger was determined to put the army back on its feet, and he too found inspiration from *On War*. In November 1984 he laid down criteria for the use of American troops abroad: 'As Clausewitz wrote, "No one starts a war – or rather, no one in his senses ought to do so – without first being clear in his mind what he intends to achieve by that war, and how he intends to conduct it."'[3] Failing to do this in Vietnam was, in Powell's words, 'mistake number one'. It 'led to Clausewitz's rule number two. Political leaders must set a war's objectives, while armies achieve them.'

Powell and Weinberger were attracted to Clausewitz precisely because he seemed to be so clear about the relationship between war and policy. However, in 1989 the collapse of the Soviet Union left the political context fluid and even opaque. Powell was appointed Chairman of the Joint Chiefs of Staff just as the United States' military found itself without an equal. In 1992, as Bosnian Serbs slaughtered Muslims in the former Yugoslavia, America's public called for its government to use military intervention. Powell's reaction was to reiterate the Weinberger doctrine, stressing the need for clear political objectives before American ground troops were committed in the Balkans. But he went further: he rejected the use of 'limited force', stating that 'decisive means and results are always to be preferred'.[4] This too was a sentiment whose origins were Clausewitzian.

The American army's other intellectual response to defeat in Vietnam had been to rethink its operational doctrine for the conduct of war, a process in which it took the German army as a model. Between 1871 and 1945 the German general staff had embraced what it called a 'strategy of annihilation', the achievement of a victory on the battlefield so decisive and so speedy that it would determine the political outcome. It was an idea which it traced to Clausewitz. Therefore two currents – one embracing the political purpose of war and the other the way it should be fought, but both drawing on a Clausewitzian pedigree – converged in the Powell doctrine of 1992. In the ensuing decade, the US army, increasingly conscious of its military superiority, focused on the second current, 'decisive means and results', to the exclusion of the first. The planning of the Iraq War of 2003 revealed that an updated version of the German 'strategy of annihilation' had subsumed Clausewitz's 'rule number one', as ironically Colin Powell – now Secretary of State – discovered. Tommy Franks, Commander-in-Chief of the United States Central Command, was almost wilful in his pursuit of rapid operational success at the expense of long-term political goals. For him 'the maxims of the Prussian strategist Carl von Clausewitz had dictated that mass – concentrated formations of troops and guns – was the key to victory. To achieve victory, Clausewitz advised, a military power must mass its forces at the enemy's "center of gravity".'[5]

Franks had been a one-star general in Operation Desert Storm, the war against Iraq in 1990–91. Then the forces of the United States and its allies had been able to apply the operational doctrine developed after Vietnam, and designed to counter the Soviet Union in the 1980s, to devastating effect. The question that dominated the aftermath of Desert Storm was whether its success pointed forwards or backwards. For Franks and others, focused on the operational dimension, it pointed forwards. New technologies would enable the American army to do even better next time. Franks thought that he was correcting Clausewitz (but that just showed that he had not read *On War* very carefully), when he concluded that, 'the victory in Desert Storm proved that speed has a mass of its own'. Others went even further, arguing that developments in information technology would remove the fog and uncertainty that surrounded the battlefield – what Clausewitz had called friction. It was precisely this concept that had so appealed to Michael Howard's own military experience.

Franks and his ilk saw themselves as refining Clausewitz, not rejecting him. But others – those who thought the influence of Desert Storm was retrograde – deemed *On War* to have lost its relevance. They detected changes not just in the character of war, but in its very nature. In 1991, Martin van Creveld published a book whose American edition was entitled *The Transformation of War*, and which his publishers dubbed 'the most radical reinterpretation of armed conflict since Clausewitz'. With the end of the Cold War the

Clausewitzian presumption that war is an act of force designed to fulfil the objects of policy was increasingly challenged. Clausewitz, so the argument runs, identified war with the state, not least because he presumed that only states have policies. Many of the conflicts waged since 1990 have been fought by non-state actors. Some of them fight for political objectives but do not employ the sorts of armies which Clausewitz described: instead, their tools are guerrillas and terrorists. Others wage war but not for political objectives, using conflict to mask organized crime, drug-running and money-laundering. For them the object is not peace (as it was for Clausewitz) but more war. By the late 1990s van Creveld might reasonably maintain that he had been vindicated. Mary Kaldor's *New and Old Wars*, published in 1999, drew a distinction between 'old wars', which were those that Clausewitz had studied, and the 'new wars' being waged by warlords in the Balkans, whose interests demanded the continuation of conflict, not its conclusion. For van Creveld and Kaldor, Bosnia represented what war had become, and Powell – in keeping the United States out of it because he wished to wage an 'old war' – was trapped in a typological confusion for which Clausewitz was responsible. Van Creveld took exception to what he called the 'Clausewitzian universe', not just because 'it rests on the assumption that war is made predominantly by states or, to be exact, by governments', but also because of Clausewitz's vision of war as 'trinitarian'. Like Powell and Summers, van Creveld described Clausewitz's trinity as made up of people, government and army. As we shall see, Clausewitz's trinity was not quite like that. Moreover, how central it was to the overall picture of war which animated *On War* in its entirety is open to question, as are both the relationship between war and policy and exactly what Clausewitz understood by policy.

Controversy is not new to Clausewitz; indeed, he invited it. In *On War* he took specific aim at one easy target and one difficult one. The easy one was an officer of the Prussian army, Adam Heinrich Dietrich von Bülow, who had endeavoured, not always very successfully, to explain the impact of the French Revolution of 1789 on the conduct of war. Bülow was declared insane in 1806 and died in 1807. He was not around to defend his corner in 1832. Antoine-Henri Jomini was, and indeed lived on until 1869, dying at the age of ninety. If modern strategic thought finds its roots in the nineteenth century, Jomini has a much greater claim to be its father than Clausewitz. A Swiss by nationality, he served as a staff officer with the French army of Napoleon between 1805 and 1813, writing as he went, and then devoting the rest of his career to refining his thoughts about warfare. The military academies and staff colleges that mushroomed in his lifetime and which were themselves symptomatic of the growing professional self-regard of soldiers proved ready consumers of his precepts.

Clausewitz's specific blows against Jomini in *On War* were few and glancing, rebutting what Jomini laid down as general principles. But he could be much more forthright in his other works, and became more so as he grew older. In an essay written in 1817, Clausewitz criticized both Bülow and Jomini for their development of 'fantastic and one-sided systems'.[6] One of Clausewitz's last pieces of historical writing was an account of the 1796 French campaign against the Austrians in Italy, when the young Napoleon had revealed his incipient military genius. The campaign became the departure point for Jomini's own analysis of how Napoleon had changed the methods of war from those of his eighteenth-century predecessors. Clausewitz said of it, on the opening page of his own account, that Jomini's 'narrative is insufficient, full of gaps, obscure, contradictory – in short it is everything that an overall account of events and their relationships should not be'.[7]

In all probability Clausewitz had not even crossed Jomini's horizon until these words were published in 1833, two years after Clausewitz's death, but Jomini rose to the challenge. In 1838 the Preface to his *Précis de l'art de la guerre,* whose qualities as a textbook established a pattern for works on strategy which has persisted until today, stated that Clausewitz has 'an easy pen' (significantly the French word was *facile*). 'But this pen,' Jomini went on, 'sometimes a little wayward, is in particular too pretentious for a didactic discussion, where simplicity and clarity must be the first requirement. More than that, the author reveals himself to be too sceptical in relation to military science: his first volume is only a blast against every theory of war, while the two following volumes, full of theoretical maxims, prove that the author believes in the efficacy of his own doctrines, even if he does not believe in those of others. As for me, I aver that I have been able to find in this labyrinthine intellect only a few insights and noteworthy points; and far from having caused me to share the author's scepticism, no work has contributed more than his to make me aware of the necessity and usefulness of good theories.'[8]

Jomini's criticisms of Clausewitz are worth quoting at length, precisely because they have never been wholly dismissed. Between 1834, when the last of the three volumes of *On War* was published, and 1871, Clausewitz was little read outside his native Prussia. Partly this was a consequence of his having written in German, a less accessible language to the literati of Europe than French. A Belgian artillery officer, Neuens, translated *On War* into French in 1849–51, and La Barre Duparcq, an instructor at St Cyr, France's military academy, then wrote a commentary on the text in 1853. Duparcq's reactions mirrored those of Jomini. He thought *On War* contained many insights but peddled false judgements and lacked overall clarity. For Clausewitz's fellow Prussians there were plenty of other works to read, even if none matched the ambition of his conception. When the publishers of *On War* somewhat optimistically decided to bring out a second and revised edition in 1853, the first printing of 1,500 copies had still not sold out. In 1857, a famous military commentator of the day, Wilhelm Rüstow, while comparing Clausewitz to Thucydides and saying he was 'good for all times', confessed that he 'has become well known, but is very little read'.[9]

Like Jomini's judgement, Rüstow's has never lost its force. However, Prussia's stunning and rapid victories over Austria in 1866 and France in 1870–71, culminating in the unification of Germany, inaugurated the first true discovery of Clausewitz. The German army now became the model for Europe, and Clausewitz was cast as its intellectual father. *On War* was translated into English by J. J. Graham in 1873. Four more German editions of *On War* were published before the First World War, and the fifth, published in 1905, had a Foreword by the Chief of the General Staff, Alfred von Schlieffen. Six editions appeared during the war itself, together with a host of abridged versions and short guides.

It is not at all clear why this should have been the case. In his old age, the architect of Prussia's victories, Helmuth von Moltke, included *On War* in a small clutch of books which had influenced him, alongside more predictable titles such as the Bible and the works of Homer. It became axiomatic that Clausewitz was Moltke's spiritual father. But there is no evidence to suggest that their paths crossed when Moltke was at the War Academy in the 1820s; although Clausewitz was its director, he did not teach. As Chief of the General Staff, Moltke trained his officers through practical exercises like staff rides and war games, not through works of theory. Certainly, if Moltke took anything from *On War*, it was not the precepts on war's relationship to policy or its 'trinitarian' nature in the terms which they came to be understood by Colin Powell or Martin van Creveld. Famously, Moltke rebutted the efforts of Prussia's Minister President (and Germany's first Chancellor), Otto von Bismarck, to assert the primacy of policy during the course of the Franco–Prussian war, claiming that policy's influence was decisive only at the opening and at the end of a conflict. 'Strategy has no choice but to strive for the highest goal attainable with the means given,' he said in 1871. 'The best way in which strategy can cooperate with diplomacy is by working solely for political ends but doing so with complete independence of action.'[10] Prussia achieved a crushing victory over Napoleon III at Sedan on 1 September 1870 but the war was prolonged until 10 May 1871. With the fall of Napoleon, the Third Republic resolved to wage a war of national resistance. Moltke's response to this intervention by the people was not to recognize the war's 'trinitarian' nature but to do his best to deny it – to say that France's guerrillas flouted the laws of war and to affirm that in Germany's own case the army, although it was conscripted, should embrace an ethos that derived not from the people but from the monarchy and its officer corps.

Gerhard Ritter, the great historian of German militarism, concluded that Moltke's conceptions, 'despite the fact that they deliberately hark back to certain formulations by Carl von Clausewitz... represent a clear departure from Clausewitz's basic views'. During the siege of Paris, in the winter of 1870–71, when the clash between Bismarck and Moltke reached its height, Moltke declared 'political elements merit consideration only to the extent that they do not make demands that are militarily improper or impossible'.[11] This was an opinion that was indeed incompatible with the parts of *On War* on which Ritter and subsequent commentators have focused – that is the first and last of its eight books, and in particular the first book's first chapter. It is here that the most cogent expression of war's relationship to policy is to be found, and it is this chapter which concludes with the 'trinity'. Moltke and his contemporaries read the intervening books of *On War* just as – if not more – carefully, precisely because they described the Napoleonic wars whose paradigm (not least thanks to Jomini) dominated military thought until 1914. The wars of German unification were short, sharp and decisive. That was both a Napoleonic and a Clausewitzian ideal. Battle settled strategy. What Moltke and his immediate successors understood by strategy was exclusively military, somewhat closer to today's usage of 'the operational level of war'. It was here that the key debates about military theory took place between 1871 and 1914. Strategy was what generals and their staffs did (and they, after all, were the most likely readers of a big book on war); it underpinned manoeuvres and exercises; and it guided the plans with which they embarked on hostilities in 1914 itself. In 1866 and 1870 Moltke had achieved decisive success because his armies had converged on the battlefield from different directions, so taking his opponents in the flank and rear as well as from the front. Although Napoleon had done the same thing, not least in his early campaigns in Italy, Clausewitz did not endorse the use of what soldiers call envelopment. In this he and Jomini were at one, and the latter – still alive in 1866, if not in 1870 – criticized Prussia's conduct of the war with Austria for that very reason. Moltke engaged with *On War* because he engaged with, and decided to modify, classical strategy, not policy. Writing in 1871, Moltke concluded in one of the rare passages where he cited Clausewitz directly: 'General von Clausewitz... said "Strategy is the use of the engagement for the goal of the war". In fact, strategy affords tactics the means for fighting and the probability of winning by the direction of armies and their meeting at the place of combat. On the one hand, strategy appropriates the success of every engagement and builds upon it. The demands of strategy grow silent in the face of a tactical victory and adapt themselves to the newly created situation.'[12]

Moltke and his successors saw *On War* as a discussion as much of the relationship between tactics, or what armies do on the battlefield, and strategy, or the use of the results they achieve on the battlefield, as of that between war and policy. And they were not wrong. In particular, Clausewitz's attention to issues of morale and courage, of will and insight, seemed even more relevant in the tactical conditions of the late nineteenth century than they had been at its beginning. Industrialization had transformed the battlefield into a fire-swept zone, traversed by breech-loading rifles, machine guns and quick-firing artillery. It had also sucked populations out of the countryside into the big cities. There, the combination of slum-dwelling, vicious leisure pursuits and urban decadence seemed to be breeding people that were unfit, both physically and psychologically, for the rigours of war.

France's love affair with Clausewitz made these points even more obvious than did Germany's. As the defeated power after 1871, France had more cause to look at the sources of Germany's success than did Germany itself. In 1885 Lucien Cardot lectured on Clausewitz at the École de Guerre, and in 1886–7 Lieutenant Colonel de Vatry produced a fresh translation of *On War* but significantly only of Books 3 to 6, those most concerned with Napoleonic warfare and those in which Vatry himself reckoned strategic principles were most clearly enunciated. These were not the books of *On War* which so impressed Colin Powell or which underpinned Martin van Creveld's 'Clausewitzian universe'. Vatry did go on to translate the rest of *On War*, but significantly Clausewitz's best-known French interpreter of the period, Georges Gilbert, said that he need not have bothered. In 1890 Gilbert declared that Clausewitzian theory could be summarized in three laws: to act simultaneously with all forces concentrated; to act quickly and most often with a direct blow; and to act without pause.[13]

Among Cardot's and Gilbert's auditors at the École de Guerre was the man who in 1918 would command the combined French, British and American forces on the Western Front in the First World War, Ferdinand Foch. In a series of lectures delivered at the École de Guerre in 1901, Foch said that the defeat in 1871 had woken the French to the fact that the nature of war was to be understood through history, that this was the method that Clausewitz had used, and that 'in the book of History, carefully analysed', Clausewitz had found 'the living Army, troops in movement and action, with their human needs, passions, weaknesses, self-denials, capacities of all sorts'. Moral forces and will power were crucial to victory. However, because both sides aspired to superiority in these respects, the enemy 'will only consider himself beaten when he is no longer able to fight: that is, when his army shall have been materially and morally destroyed'. 'Therefore', Foch was able to conclude, 'modern war can only consider those arguments which lead to the destruction of that army: namely battle, overthrow by force.'[14] Clausewitz expressed himself in just such terms, as Foch himself demonstrated by direct quotation.

This was the Clausewitz to whom the British military commentator Basil Liddell Hart would take such strong exception after the First World War. During the war Foch put into practice what he preached, or at least he never specifically retracted it. Foch, Liddell Hart wrote in 1931 in a biography of the French marshal, 'had caught only Clausewitz's strident generalizations, and not his subtler undertones'. Thus Liddell Hart's Clausewitz was one mediated by the generals of the First World War. The implication in his criticism of Foch was that there was another Clausewitz. But if he really believed that, he never acted on it. In Liddell Hart's mind the guts of the problem lay not with Foch, but with Clausewitz himself: 'The ponderous tomes of Clausewitz are so solid as to cause mental indigestion to any student who swallows them without a long course of preparation. Only a mind developed by years of study and reflection can dissolve the solid lump into digestible particles.'[15] In his Lees Knowles lectures, delivered at Cambridge in 1932–3, Basil Liddell Hart blamed Clausewitz for the slaughter of the First World War, memorably but somewhat meaninglessly dubbing him 'the Mahdi of Mass'. He declared that, 'Clausewitz's principle of force without limit and without calculation of cost fits, and is only fit for, a hate-maddened mob. It is the negation of statesmanship – and of intelligent strategy, which seeks to serve the ends of policy.'[16]

If Liddell Hart had been right, there would have been no need for Martin van Creveld and others to have declared Clausewitz dead after the Cold War; he would already have been knocked from his pedestal after the First World War. Indeed, in France and Britain (where his perch had in any case been much rockier) he was. But that did not apply in his homeland.

Defeat in 1918 prompted Germans to return to Clausewitz, not to ditch him. This time round, however, they read him in different ways. The second discovery of Clausewitz was pioneered less by soldiers, as had been the case after 1871, than by academics. Before the First World War, Hans Delbrück, himself a veteran of the Franco–Prussian War and a professor in Berlin, had argued that, if Clausewitz had lived, he would have gone on to develop a system for strategy that would have recognized two different forms of waging war. The first would have been a strategy of annihilation. The second would have been a strategy designed to wear the enemy out, so that he would agree to negotiate. Delbrück had argued, somewhat tendentiously, that the king of Prussia, Frederick the Great, had tried to do the second of these in the Seven Years War between 1756 and 1763, an interpretation vigorously contested by the historians of the General Staff. In some respects, both sides were reflecting the preoccupations of their own callings. Delbrück was looking at strategy in a political context; Frederick sought a negotiated peace because Austria was confronted by an alliance of France, Russia and Prussia, and so was not strong enough to hope for more. The General Staff conceived of strategy in a military or operational light: for them Frederick sought battle, not shunned it, especially when it gave him the opportunity to deal with one of his enemies in isolation. The German army entered the First World War convinced that there was only one way to fight a war, and that way was the strategy of annihilation resulting in complete German victory: its operational thought was scaled up to the level of policy.

Delbrück maintained a running commentary on the war

as it unfolded and after it was over renewed his attacks on the army's approach to strategy – and especially on Erich Ludendorff, the de facto head of the German army between 1916 and 1918. What Delbrück's extrapolations from *On War* brought out was the role of dialectics in Clausewitzian thought. Books 3 to 5 of *On War*, those on which many military theorists of 1871 to 1914 had concentrated, described a unitary conception of war, predominantly derived from the Napoleonic wars and concerned with strategy in an operational sense; both the beginning of *On War*, Books 1 and 2, and the end, Books 6, 7 and 8, allowed for alternatives. Even as the First World War ended, a youthful German scholar, Hans Rothfels, was putting the finishing touches to his doctoral thesis on Clausewitz's early career and its role in the formulation of his ideas. The parallel seemed direct. In 1806, Prussia was defeated by France. Clausewitz had found himself in the same position as many young Germans in 1918. His own life and times therefore became important to the interpretation of his work. *On War* was not to be read as a staff college manual, in bits, but as a whole, and it was to be seen in the context of the philosophical ideas which underpinned it. At the operational level, this involved the rediscovery of Book 6, with its declaration that the defence was stronger than the offence, a precept with particular resonance for those who had fought in the trenches in 1914–18, and who also found fresh merit in Clausewitz's description of battle as a form of attrition. But the most important consequence of this spate of activity, and particularly of Rothfels's own work, was the reconsideration of what Clausewitz had said about the relationship between war and policy.

The German army convinced itself that it had not lost the First World War, but that in November 1918 revolution at home had precipitated defeat. The so-called 'stab in the back' led it to pay more attention to the third element of Clausewitz's 'trinity', the people. Ludendorff recognized that war now involved the full mobilization of the entire resources of the nation. In a book published in 1922, *Kriegführung und Politik*, Ludendorff began with a respectful discussion of Clausewitz's ideas, which said (not quite accurately) that for Clausewitz policy meant only foreign policy, not domestic policy, but that the First World War, which for Germany was a war for existence, showed that references to policy in *On War* should now be understood to apply to both. Moreover, as his title made clear, the conduct of war, *Kriegführung*, should be put ahead of policy: the latter should serve the former, and not vice versa. In *Der totale Krieg*, which appeared in 1935, he went further. The proper translation of this title is not 'total war', but, as the English edition (which is called *The Nation at War*) makes clear, 'totalitarian war'. Ludendorff's attention was not on how to wage war against an enemy in the operational sense, but on how to mobilize the whole state for war. 'All the theories of Clausewitz should be thrown overboard,' he wrote. 'Both warfare and politics are meant to serve the preservation of the people, but warfare is the highest expression of the national "will to live", and politics must, therefore, be subservient to the conduct of war.'[17]

Ironically, therefore, Ludendorff joined Liddell Hart in blaming the conduct of the First World War on Clausewitz. For Ludendorff, the problem was that the First World War was so different from earlier wars that *On War* had saddled Germany with a conception of war's nature that was too limited. Liddell Hart on the one hand wanted to demolish Clausewitz because he wanted to restrict war; Ludendorff on the other wanted to abandon him because he wanted to widen the scope of policy: 'like the totalitarian war, politics, too, must assume a totalitarian character'.[18] Ludendorff therefore acted as a bridge between the ideas of the German General Staff in 1914–18 and the rhetoric of Fascism. By eroding the distinctions between war and peace, and defining politics as an existential struggle for survival, the Nazis imported the vocabulary of war to daily life. But, contrary to Ludendorff's beliefs, totalitarianism did not imply the death of Clausewitz. Karl Haushofer, the professor of geopolitics at Munich and himself a National Socialist, delivered a copy of *On War* to the political prisoners held in Landsberg prison after the failed Nazi *Putsch* of 1924. In 1933, as the Nazis seized power, he wrote to one of them, Rudolf Hess, 'Remember the word of Clausewitz, so that you yourself can rouse the German nation to life again.'[19] The Clausewitz who appealed to the Nazis was less the theorist of war whom Ludendorff rejected and more the spokesman of an existential conflict with Napoleonic France, whom the academics had discovered but Ludendorff had overlooked. 'Not all of you may have read Clausewitz, and, if you have read it you have not understood it and realized how to apply it to the future,' Adolf Hitler told an audience in Munich on 9 November 1934. 'Clausewitz writes that recovery is still always possible after a heroic collapse... It is always better, indeed necessary, to embrace an end with horror than to suffer horror without end.'[20]

In April 1945, less than nine years later, these words would acquire an awful reality for the German nation as the Red Army closed on Berlin. Hitler did indeed embrace 'an end with horror' in a battle which represented the clash of two contrasting interpretations of Clausewitz's thinking on the relationship between war and policy. *On War* was not translated into Russian until 1902, and inadequately even then. But a fresh version appeared in 1932–3, and it had reached its fifth Russian edition by the time of the German invasion of Russia in 1941. The appeal of Clausewitz to totalitarian governments was therefore confirmed by his reception in the Soviet Union. In 1858 the founding father of Communism, Karl Marx, had written of Clausewitz, that 'the fellow has a common sense that borders on wit'.[21] The Bolshevik party leader, V. I. Lenin, was particularly taken by Clausewitz's formulation that war was waged for the ends of policy and made extensive use of *On War* when he wrote his essay on socialism and war while in exile in Switzerland in 1915. After the Russian Revolutions of 1917, Lenin's chief executive, Leon Trotsky, tried to balance the political imperatives of revolutionary socialism with military realities as he set about the creation of the Red Army. For him, the dialectical approach of Books 1 and 8 held a particular appeal: 'We must reject all attempts at building an absolute revolutionary strategy with the elements of our limited experience of three years of civil war during which army sections of a special quality engaged in combat under special conditions. Clausewitz has warned very correctly against this.'[22]

The symmetry between Marxism–Leninism and Clausewitz was challenged by the bitter fighting of the Russo–German war of 1941–5. By 1945 Clausewitz laboured under three besetting sins in Russian eyes: first, he was German, and therefore his ideas were those of the enemy; second, German military thought had been responsible for two world wars; and third, the German way of war had proved remarkably unsuccessful in both, resulting in successive and resounding defeats. The problem of Lenin's enthusiasm for *On War* was dealt with by explaining that he never addressed the specifically military side of Clausewitz's thinking. What appealed to Lenin was the observation that war was a continuation of policy, but that attracted him because he was a Marxist, and Clausewitz, self-evidently, was not. In February 1946, the party leader, Josef Stalin, declared that Clausewitz was out of date, 'a representative of the age of manufactures in war', whereas 'now we stand in the machine age of war'.[23]

Once again Clausewitz seemed to be dead and buried, and indeed to all intents and purposes in the Soviet Union he was – at least until Stalin was. But in 1956, the year in which Nikita Khrushchev's speech to the twentieth party congress condemned not only the policies of his predecessor, Stalin, but also his conduct of the war in its opening phases in 1941, Clausewitz's rehabilitation in Soviet military thought began. Using Lenin to legitimate their own thinking, Soviet military writers sought to integrate the destructiveness of nuclear weapons within the framework of inevitable class struggle. They argued that war was both a tool of policy – in the sense that policy initiates war and determines its objectives – and that policy governs strategy, so shaping the way that the war is conducted. Marxism–Leninism made Soviet soldiers the purest of Clausewitzians, even to the point of accepting their own subordination to political authority, on the understanding that the government itself comprehended the nature of the military instrument that was at its disposal. However, there was also an implicit split between Soviet strategic thought, which incorporated nuclear weapons within mainstream military doctrine, and Soviet policy, which recognized that their destructive effects could outstrip any political gain. As the Soviet dissident Andrei Sakharov recognized, nuclear weapons seemed to invalidate all the standard propositions put forward by the fusion of Marxism–Leninism and Clausewitz: 'if Clausewitz's formula were applied across the board in our day and age, we would be dealing not with the "continuation of politics by other means" but with the total self-destruction of civilization'.[24]

Therefore, at its height the Cold War suggested that war could not be the means to fulfil the objectives of policy. However, again the text of *On War* provided its own basis for Clausewitz's resurrection. German scholars, like Gerhard Ritter, anxious to discard the Nazis' appropriation of Clausewitz in explaining and justifying 'total war', argued that in *On War* 'politics in no way appears as the intensifying element, but as the moderating'.[25] In France, Raymond Aron used Clausewitz's interest in dialectics to follow through the logic of his own arguments, left unfinished by his death in 1831. In *Penser la guerre, Clausewitz*, published in 1976, Aron extrapolated from the implications of Book 6 of *On War*, which stated that defence is stronger than offence, to conclude that Clausewitz would have gone on to develop a theory of conflict resolution: the war-mongering Prussian was being transmogrified into a liberal theorist of international relations.

Nuclear deterrence gave the threat of war, rather than war itself, a political utility, and so could be treated in Clausewitzian terms. Moreover, limited wars were being waged under the nuclear umbrella. Here the salience of political utility was even more marked than in the major wars that had characterized most of Clausewitz's analysis. In *The Nuclear Question*, published in 1979, Michael Mandelbaum began with Clausewitz's conception of 'absolute war', a phrase Clausewitz originally coined to characterize the Napoleonic wars, to show that 'the logic of war, as Clausewitz defined it, is Hiroshima'. But he then went on to say that 'real wars do not become absolute. There are natural barriers that limit war's violence. And there is a man-made barrier as well; the political control of force.'[26] The role of policy in relation to war was now to enable the waging of limited, not major, war. Clausewitz's legacy was being appropriated not by Nazis or Bolsheviks, but by the democratic states of the West.

The translation used by Mandelbaum was that of Howard and Paret. They themselves acknowledged that translation requires interpretation. As this Introduction has endeavoured to show, *On War* is open to many. With the Cold War at its height, Howard and Paret gave priority to Clausewitz the rationalist, who stressed the relationship between war and policy, with the implication at times that policy can be equated with the policies of liberal democracies. In invading Iraq in 2003, President Bush made clear that his policy goals included the idea that war should be used to advance democracy. Those who see the ideological objectives of the 2003 war in Iraq as the continued pursuit of a Cold War agenda can also find in that war evidence of the uses to which *On War* has been put in the United States. However, as the war struggles to achieve its objectives, and as the Bush government's policy is itself challenged, the consensus around which the 'liberal' Clausewitz was created is thrown into doubt. Clausewitz's claim to contemporary relevance has more than the prevalence of civil wars and of conflicts between non-state actors with which to contend.

It does not matter in the present context whether any of these pictures is overdrawn or not. The key issue is that those who now reject Clausewitz, like all those who have done so in the past, do so on the basis of a selective reading of a vast body of material. *On War* is itself unfinished: the text which we have is a work in progress and its judgements are not consistent. That is the very source of its enduring strength. As Stewart Murray, one of a legion of hacks tempted to produce abbreviated versions of *On War*, wrote in 1909: 'It is perhaps this unfinished state which renders Clausewitz so essentially in touch with, and a part of, the onward movement and evolution of military thought.'[27] Murray was more right than perhaps he knew. Moreover, behind *On War* is a mass of other material, some of it political, most of it military. Clausewitz's other writings are not separate from *On War*. They are the rock from which the magnum opus was carved – or, perhaps a more appropriate metaphor, the anvil on which the ideas were forged.

The primary purpose of the present book is to understand the origins of Clausewitz's thoughts, their evolution and the varied forms in which they manifest themselves in his most important book. Only if this is done is it possible to understand how he thought about war, as opposed to how others have elected to interpret those thoughts. The issues are complex. Those who have simplified *On War* have done a great disservice, not just because they have been selective and self-serving in their judgements but also because they have lost the richness of a text whose range continues to astonish. The most important task is to return to what he wrote himself, and to put it in the context of his own times, not ours. Once the many different ways in which Clausewitz saw war are clear, then it will be possible to see what particular facets of his thought appealed to those who came after him and who said they were influenced by him. The ultimate point is that neither Hitler nor Marx was wrong: there was something in Clausewitz for each of them. The same goes for both democrats and warlords today. Each generation has read Clausewitz differently, often selectively, but not necessarily inaccurately.

CHAPTER 1

The Reality of War

For a man now best known as an author, Clausewitz was remarkably cynical about the genre in which he was to establish his posthumous reputation. He accused his contemporaries who wrote about war of those very failings with which he himself has been charged – vagueness, mystification, abstraction and pseudo-science. His concern, he stressed repeatedly, was to keep his analysis rooted in reality. 'Just as some plants bear fruit only if they don't shoot up too high', he declared in a Preface to an unpublished work on war written between 1816 and 1818, 'so in the practical arts the leaves and flowers of theory must be pruned and the plant kept close to its proper soil – experience.'[1]

Clausewitz was able to deliver precisely because his own experience of war was so intense and so pervasive. He served throughout the wars of the French Revolution and of Napoleon, from 1792 until 1815, the most prolonged and violent series of conflicts to assail Europe between the Thirty Years War (1618–48) and the First World War (1914–18), and for many commentators (including Clausewitz himself) the foundation of modem war. 'My entry to the world was to an arena of great opportunities, in which the fate of nations would be decided,' he wrote to his fiancée, Marie von Brühl, in 1807. 'Thus my gaze fell not on the temple in which domesticity celebrates its quiet good fortune, but on the triumphal arch through which the victor passes when the fresh laurel wreath cools his glowing brow.'[2]

That did not happen: Clausewitz never became the conquering hero. His lust for glory outstripped his achievements. He lived in the age of Napoleon, Wellington and, from Prussia itself, Gebhard von Blücher, but he was younger than they; too young to achieve high rank in the wars in which he took part, even if he had deserved it. He confessed that his constant sense of dissatisfaction, of lack of fulfilment, might well have been attributable to thwarted ambition. He would rather have exercised high command than written about it. None the less, he was not a professional failure. By the age of thirty-eight he had become a major-general. Moreover, he found his vocation in war. Military service in peacetime gave him little satisfaction. He would have preferred, if he could have afforded it (which he could not), to have retired to the country to study and write.[3] He made his motives for being a soldier clear in a letter to Marie on 1 September 1807: 'If men have degraded our manly honour, then men must also be able to regain it; I don't mean through the conditions of peace and its weak means; war opens a broad field for energetic means, and if I am frank about the innermost thoughts of my soul, for me they are the most mighty of all; I would arouse the lazy beasts with cracks of the whip and teach them to break the shackles in which they have let themselves be placed by cowardice and fear.'[4]

Clausewitz's chilling words, the suggestion that war purges decadence and revitalizes national life, resonate beyond his own times, pointing forward to the ideas of Fascism. However, the context in which he penned them was specific. He had just heard the terms of the treaty of Tilsit, the confirmation of Prussia's abject humiliation at the hands of France on the battlefield the year before. His homeland had been stripped of half its population and a third of its territory, and the army in which he served was reduced to a sixth of its former size. Later in life, reflecting in peacetime on the course of military history, he was able to see what individual circumstance meant for attempts to generalize about the nature of war. 'Every age has had its own peculiar forms of war, its own restrictive conditions, and its own prejudices,' he wrote in Book 8, Chapter 3, of *On War*. 'Each, therefore, would also keep its own theory of war, even if everywhere, in early times as well as in later, there had been an inclination to work it out on philosophical principles. The events of each age must, therefore, be judged with due regard to the peculiarities of the time, and only he who, less by an anxious study of minute details than by a shrewd glance at the main features, can place himself in each particular age is able to understand and appreciate its generals.'[5]

To comprehend *On War*, it too has to be placed in the context in which it was written. It is first and foremost a response to one man's experience and to the wars through which he lived and in which he served.

Carl Clausewitz was born on 1 June 1780 [6] in Burg, close to Magdeburg. His grandfather was professor of theology at Halle. Both his great-grandfather and great-great grandfather were Lutheran pastors, themselves married to daughters of the clergy, and this was the calling for which one of Carl's elder brothers also prepared. Clausewitz's wife believed his gifts were God-given.[7] 'Religion', he wrote to Marie, 'should not take our gaze from this world; it is a heavenly power which walks in step with the noble things of life, and religious feeling has never yet run through me and strengthened me without inspiring me to good deeds, without giving me a wish – yes, even a hope – of something greater than me.'[8] However, Clausewitz himself made little reference to religion and less to his own beliefs in his writings. He displayed the almost unconscious anti-Semitism of his times.[9] Faith was not cited as a motivation for war or in war; Christianity was not seen as an impulse for moderation in fighting fellow Christians, or for excesses against those of other religions. But in 1807 he visited Reims Cathedral, and, although his initial reactions were historical and architectural, its Gothic splendours moved him to spiritual reflection and to admiration of the patterns of Christian worship. 'The greatness of the founder, who has awakened these sentiments in the bulk of the human race, is astounding, at a time when false doctrines on the one hand and barbarous brutality on the other appear more than ever to have distanced it from mankind.'[10] *On War* makes full use of analogies drawn from Clausewitz's eclectic readings across other fields of human endeavour – pre-eminently philosophy, but also the law, the sciences, the arts; unsurprisingly, but less obviously, the text is also marked by the scriptures on which Clausewitz was raised.

Much more direct an influence on the young Clausewitz than the Church was the army. 'I am a son of the camp, but from a real one, not from Schiller's poetic world like Max Piccolomini,' Carl told Marie.[11] In 1786, when Frederick the Great died, nine-tenths of Prussian officers were noble; among those whose names enjoyed the right to the prefix 'von' was Marie's own family. Clausewitz's did not. Carl was clearly sensitive on the point: to impress his inamorata, he created a bogus lineage, designed to show that he was sprung from Silesian aristocracy. In fact, his father had served as a junior officer in the Prussian army during the Seven Years War (1756–63), but precisely because he was not noble he had been retired when the size of the officer corps was cut back after the war. He used the title 'von' because he had been an officer; not until 1827 would his family's entitlement to it be formally sanctioned by the king.

At the time of his birth, Clausewitz's father was a minor official. However, Burg was the town where the regiment in which he had passed his wartime service was quartered. In Clausewitz's own words, 'he grew up in the Prussian army'.[12] His father's old comrades frequented the house, and the talk was of soldiering. They were entitled to rest on their laurels. The Prussian army was the admiration of Europe. In 1756 it had faced a coalition of Austria, France and Russia, the first of whom had been determined to reconquer Silesia, seized by Frederick the Great on his accession to the throne of Prussia in 1740, and possibly even to obliterate Prussia as an independent state. On 4 December 1757, the evening before the battle of Leuthen, Frederick's most comprehensive and famous victory over the Austrians, the king had told his officers that they were fighting for their homes and families. On the following evening, reflecting the Pietism in which Clausewitz was brought up, the survivors spontaneously took up the refrain of Luther's great hymn, 'Now thank we all our God'.

The Prussian army was outnumbered two to one at Leuthen and by nearly three to one by the allies that it faced in 1756. But it prevailed and Prussia survived. Despite being ranked thirteenth in Europe in terms of population, Prussia raised an army that was the fourth biggest. It did so by the canton system, a form of compulsory military service which rendered peasants liable for military obligations as well as feudal. Although, like other eighteenth-century armies, it relied also on mercenaries, especially in peacetime, this was an army with an incipient national identity. Moreover, the army was the embodiment of the state. Its commander, the outstanding general of the age, was also its king. Its campaigns expanded and defined its national frontiers. And within those frontiers the economy, the taxation system and the bureaucracy were bent to providing the infrastructure to support the state's use of military power.

When Prussia emerged, battered but in one piece, from the Seven Years War, military visitors flocked to Potsdam to see what it was that had underpinned the army's performance in the field. They marvelled at the drill and discipline which had given Frederick's forces the tactical facility to prevail on the close-order battlefield. They paid less attention to the rumblings of reform in France, whose army had been humiliated by Frederick at Rossbach a month before Leuthen. Frederick himself resisted the tactical innovations pioneered not only in campaigns outside Europe, specifically in America, but also on the continent's peripheries, in mountains, forests and uncultivated wastelands. Here troops dispersed, used cover, and fought more as individuals than as members of closely drilled units. Late eighteenth-century Prussia was even more unhappy with the political and social reforms which some argued underpinned greater tactical flexibility. The message from America was that free men fought best and did so because they were citizens.

This was an argument picked up by a French aristocrat and veteran of the Seven Years War, Jacques-Antoine-

Hippolyte, comte de Guibert, in his *Essai général de la tactique* (1770). Like others, Guibert lauded Frederick; in 1773, he made the pilgrimage to Prussia, met the king and attended manoeuvres in Breslau. But Guibert pointed forward as well as back. He was Clausewitz's most obvious immediate intellectual predecessor, although it is a link about which Clausewitz remained largely silent. Significantly, Guibert is not cited in *On War*, perhaps because most of the military theorists who are were those to whom Clausewitz took exception. But Clausewitz certainly read Guibert. In February 1812, in the third of a series of 'political declarations' designed to rally Germans against France, Clausewitz quoted in full one of Guibert's most famous passages: 'Let us suppose in Europe, there was to spring up a people, with genius, with power, and a happy form of government; a set of people that to strict virtue, and to national soldiery, joined a fixed plan of aggrandizement, who never lost sight of that system, who knowing how to carry on a war with little expence, and to subsist by their conquests, was not reduced to the necessity of laying down their arms by financiers. As the north wind bends the tender reed, those people would be seen to subjugate their neighbours, and overthrow our feeble constitutions.'[13]

Guibert went on to deny that such a people would ever appear, but he was more prescient than he realized, as Clausewitz knew full well by 1812. Very few changes in the conduct of war, according to *On War*, 'can be ascribed to new inventions or new departures in ideas'; instead, they arise 'mainly from the transformation of society and new social conditions'.[14] The basis for Clausewitz's belief was quite specific. In 1789 revolution in France maximized the power of the state through its claim that citizenship gave it an authority more complete than that exercised by absolute monarchs like Frederick and his successors. In February 1792 Prussia formed a defensive alliance with Austria, responding to the latter's commitment to the defence both of its own possessions in the Netherlands and to the German principalities in the Rhineland. In April the French attacked Austria and in June Prussia declared war on France. 'It was expected that a moderate auxiliary corps would be enough to end a civil war', Clausewitz wrote, 'but the colossal weight of the whole French people, unhinged by political fanaticism, came crushing down us.'[15]

That same spring the youthful Clausewitz was accepted into the 34th Prussian Infantry Regiment (Prince Ferdinand's), whose previous commanding officer had been his father's stepbrother, and in which one of his elder brothers was already serving. In 1793 the twelve-year-old found himself in the trenches besieging Mainz. Here the adolescent Clausewitz witnessed at first hand the clash between the armies of the old order and the new. The outstanding Austrian commander of the war, Archduke Charles, reflected a common belief when he attributed the allies' defeat not to the enemy, the French, whose military organization seemed to be chaotic, but to the internal failings of the allies themselves. Austria and Prussia were divided not just by the conduct of the war in north-west Europe but also by their competition for the territory offered by the partition of Poland. The problems of coalition warfare were to constitute a recurrent theme of *On War*. However, a Hanoverian officer of even humbler origins than Clausewitz, Gerhard Scharnhorst, concluded that the consistency of France's victories was to be found in the hearts of Frenchmen: 'they believed that they alone are enlightened, clever, free and lucky and that all other nations are backward, bovine and unlucky... They believed that they were fighting not only for their own future existence and fortune, but also for that of all mankind.'[16] In April 1795 Prussia conceded all territory on the left bank of the Rhine to France, and consoled itself with its gains in Poland and its domination of north Germany.

Prussia now enjoyed nearly a decade of peace and neutrality. As hostilities ended in the spring of 1795, Clausewitz was billeted with a Westphalian peasant family for three to four months. 'Withdrawn from war, and transferred to the calm of rural life in all its meaning, for the first time my spirit looked inwards.'[17] Nearby Osnabrück provided the books which launched the fifteen-year-old on the path of self-education. Clausewitz began with the writings of the Enlightenment, and was sufficiently drawn to philosophy to begin to doubt his vocation as a soldier. His comrades were ordinary men, content to settle into the routine of post-war garrison life in Neuruppin. However, his commanding officer reflected the spirit of the age in his belief in the value of education. He had no truck with the idea that reading and writing would make private soldiers discontented with life in the ranks, or – even worse – turn them into political radicals. On the contrary, he held that basic literacy and arithmetic would make them more proficient in their military duties. His officers, and Clausewitz above all, benefited from both his policies and his library. As well as the works of Schiller, Goethe and Hölderlin, Clausewitz began reading military history. And so the tension between this newly discovered and exciting inner world and the outer world of military ambition found some sort of reconciliation.

The process was taken a stage further in late 1801, when he entered the war school in Berlin, the Berliner Allgemeine Kriegsschule, revitalized by Scharnhorst, who had forsaken the service of Hanover for that of Prussia. The French revolutionary wars had convinced Scharnhorst that the armies of Germany had to be reformed, that they should be recruited through compulsory but universal military service, that promotion should be by merit, that education could develop talent, and that tactical innovation was predicated on social and political change. These were potentially unsettling arguments for a monarchy concerned by the spread of revolutionary ideas from France. Nor were its fears simple reflections of conservatism. The Terror, which had purged the aristocracy of France, had found its application on the battlefield: the armies, which said they brought liberty, equality and fraternity, also raped, looted and pillaged. None the less, Scharnhorst was free to teach and to set up a military discussion group, the Militärische Gesellschaft, attended by civilians as well as soldiers.

Scharnhorst's relationship with Clausewitz – at once paternal and pedagogic – was of decisive importance. Twice Clausewitz's age, he was, Clausewitz said, 'the father and friend of my intellect and of my spirit'.[18] Crucially, Clausewitz's own father had died in 1802, just as he and Scharnhorst met. Politically, Scharnhorst was not a radical, but he was a reformer, a product of the Enlightenment. France had tapped the resources of its people by revolution; Prussia could do it by giving them rights before the law, by emancipating the serfs, and by providing universal systems of education. Liberalizing Prussia would save it through reinvigoration, and the pay-off would be on the battlefield. Scharnhorst had imbibed the ideas of the Enlightenment in a military context, at the military academy of Crown Prince Wilhelm of Schaumburg-Lippe. The author of two military manuals, he emphasized the importance of theory, but taught that it should be derived from correct concepts, grounded in the nature of things and in practical experience. The role of theory was to elucidate events, and so reason alone was insufficient. Detailed military history was required to enable an understanding of the true nature of war, and should be used in the training of officers: in other words, experience, not systems or general principles, revealed the reality of war. Theory had to be concrete and circumstantial, not dogmatic and prescriptive.

Clausewitz's earliest military writings belong to this period. The stimulus not only of the war school, the military society and Scharnhorst, but also of the intellectual life of the capital city, invigorated by the ideas of the German *Aufklärung* (Enlightenment), were an intoxicating mixture for a young man entering adulthood. Personally, he was somewhat gauche, too serious minded for the frolics of his regimental colleagues, unable to make light of issues, and desperate to acquire the refinements which provincial life had so far blocked. But his writings on professional issues show no lack of assurance. War as he had experienced it bore little relationship to war as he found it laid out by the fashionable theorists of the day. In a piece on strategy written in 1804, he took aim at Bülow, whose *Geist des neuern Kriegssystems*. published in 1799, made geometry the basis of strategy. Bülow's *Lehrsätze des neuern Krieges* was the subject of Clausewitz's first published (but anonymous) work, which appeared in the journal *Neue Bellona* in 1805. Bülow, and others of his ilk, Clausewitz said, were sophists, who were 'totally incapable of developing an art on scientific principles'.[19] The forthrightness of *On War*, even its intellectual arrogance, was present in its author from the first.

He passed out top from the war school in a class of forty, one of two events in his life, or at least up until 1807, which he said gave him unalloyed joy. The other was put in train that same winter, 1803–4. He had been appointed adjutant to Prince August, the youngest son of Prince Ferdinand, the colonel-in-chief of the 34th Infantry Regiment. The post kept him in Berlin, allowing him to continue his studies; it also gave him greater means and social standing. At court he met Marie von Brühl, and by 1805 the two were in love. When in the following year Clausewitz went off to war once more, their relationship grew in intensity, fed by a correspondence which is our best insight into Clausewitz's personality and which makes clear the mutual vocabulary which not only politics but also the arts and music gave their relationship. Marie was a cultured woman who developed and widened her future husband's interests, who eased his angst and affirmed his strengths. But she was also his social superior and her widowed mother, an Englishwoman, was sufficiently conscious of that to block the marriage until 1810.

Marie's English origins were affronted by Prussia's continued neutrality as Napoleon rearranged the map of Europe. It set her at odds with the policy of the king, Friedrich Wilhelm III, who did not join a fresh coalition against France formed in 1805 by Britain, Russia and Austria. An anonymous paper on a possible war with France, attributed to Clausewitz, suggests that military pragmatism as well as economic self-interest may have contributed to this decision. Reflecting the experience of the first coalition against France and anticipating the belief in the unreliability of allies that peppers *On War*, it suggested that the alliance would not be able to produce a commander to match Napoleon and that the only way its armies would be able to operate effectively would be in their own theatres of war, in defence of their own homelands and in pursuit of their own war aims: the lack of unity of action might be mitigated by the deployment of their armies in contiguous theatres, arcing from Holland, up the Rhine, to Switzerland and Italy.[20] In the event the coalition could not achieve even this degree of coordination. Napoleon surrounded one Austrian army at Ulm in October 1805 and then advanced along the Danube and finished off the remainder of the Austrians, together with the Russians, at Austerlitz on 2 December 1805.

To many Germans, Prussia's neutrality was now a covert form of French domination. As Clausewitz later argued, Prussia under Frederick the Great had been a second-class state able to perform in the premier league because of the guile and courage of its king and the qualities of the military organization which he had crafted. But his successors lacked his spirit and by 1806 the army possessed but a 'nimbus' of its former qualities. 'The machine still made a rattle, so nobody asked whether it was capable of service.' It had conducted only a couple of campaigns in forty-five years, and those without a full commitment. It had not come to grips with the fact that since 1792 war was waged 'by the whole nation and was a matter of life and death'. By hoping that it could somehow bypass the fate of the rest of Europe, Prussia had neither reformed its army along the lines that Scharnhorst and others had been urging, nor prepared its people for the national mobilization that war in the age of the French Revolution would require. Prussia affected liberalism, as the tolerance shown the reformers testified, but it did not effect it.[21]

In the winter of 1805 and the spring of 1806 Prussia continued to duck and weave, refusing to accept that war was now a necessary instrument of policy. Austria made terms with France after Austerlitz. France offered Hanover to Prussia as a reward for its pro-French neutrality, but in accepting it Prussia made an enemy of Britain. Prussia turned to Russia, but its shattered army was in retreat. With Napoleon's troops on its frontiers, Prussia was reduced to a French pawn. Finally mobilizing part (but not all) of its army in August, on 1 October 1806 it sent an ultimatum demanding France's withdrawal. Napoleon rejected it. When Clausewitz had last gone to war he was a boy; now he went to war as an adult. It was to prove a defining experience.

'My fatherland has need of war,' he wrote to Marie on 18 September 1806, 'and – truth to tell – war alone can enable me to achieve happiness. In whatever way I wanted to connect my life to the world as a whole, my path always led me through a major battlefield.'[22] He revelled in the identification of his own life with that of the state which his appointment as a staff captain in Prince August's battalion of grenadiers gave him. He was, as he remembered after the war, 'a Prussian officer in the complete sense of the word'.[23] He knew that Prussia was unsupported, that its army had put only half its strength into the field, and that its command was divided, but the need for optimism as he and his state accepted the challenge of war inclined him to moderate his criticisms of Prussian policy. 'If I draw a conclusion from all the observations I have made,' he wrote on 29 September, 'it seems to me probable that we shall be the victors in the next great battle.'[24]

They were not. On 14 October 1806, the Frederickian army was smashed in the twin battles of Jena and Auerstädt, fifteen miles apart. Clausewitz was with the army of the Duke of Brunswick at Auerstädt, while Napoleon concentrated against the over-extended army of Prince von Hohenlohe further south at Jena. Preoccupied with securing its own lines of communication, Brunswick's force failed to defeat the detached and smaller French body which confronted it. What made Jena one of the decisive battles of history was the pursuit which followed, the strategic exploitation of tactical triumph, as Napoleon's army chased the Prussians north-eastwards. Napoleon received the capitulation of Berlin on 26 October. Two days later, Hohenlohe surrendered without a fight at Prenzlau, and the day after the fortified city of Stettin also offered no resistance. Even Blücher and Scharnhorst, who had hatched a plan to get their troops away to Britain from Lübeck, surrendered. In a campaign which lasted a month the Prussians lost 25,000 men killed and wounded, most of them on 14 October itself, but fully 140,000 were taken prisoner.

Clausewitz was among those who surrendered at Prenzlau. 'The almost complete destruction of the Prussian army has shattered the bravest,' he wrote on 19 February 1807, in the third of three letters on the campaign, 'and the sophisms of an average intellect completed the triumph of shame over honour.'[25] This letter, which was published in the same year, was written from France. At the end of December 1806 Prince August was interned by the French and Clausewitz accompanied him. As he travelled from Nancy to Soissons and then Paris, Clausewitz reported to Marie on the sights that he saw. But tourism did not oust his dislike, and increasingly hatred, of the French, whom he caricatured as vain, cruel, deceitful and frivolous, a francophobia still evident in the very last chapter of *On War*. France as a nation was right to try to extend its own power, but that did not mean that other nations should give in.

As so often in Clausewitz, there was paradox here. Napoleon was the cause of the Prussian army's downfall, but what Prussia needed was a Napoleon of its own, 'the resolution of a great man'. The king, Friedrich Wilhelm III, lacked the force of character to fulfil the nation's need. Clausewitz was careful not to traduce in print the monarch to whom, as a soldier, he was bound to serve, but the divergence between the will of the monarch and the needs of the nation left Clausewitz with a dilemma that ultimately proved irreconcilable. The problem was personal as well as public: Clausewitz described himself on 1 December 1806 as unable to separate his fate and his hopes from those of his fatherland. His reaction was to shift the focus of his patriotism from Prussia and its dynasty to Germany and its nation. Prussia had failed to match the hopes of all Germany, he declared in the peroration to his third letter, but that was itself a challenge. 'We need to double our courage to bear the misfortune and shame of the moment for the nation! And yet I can call on all Germans: take pride in yourselves, that is: do not doubt your fate!'[26]

The verdict of Jena was therefore not final. Clausewitz drew an analogy with medicine, where the young doctor confronted an illness which could go in either direction. The doctor could not intervene but he would be wrong to declare the patient to be incurable. He could only wait on nature, which itself seemed to stimulate the body to fight back. This was, for a doctor, the meaning of crisis, the point at which things could go either way. For Clausewitz also, it was too soon to say that all hope was lost.[27] He returned to Prussia in November 1807, ready to take part in the regeneration of the state and its army.

That had begun. In July the king gave responsibility for the direction of domestic and foreign affairs to Heinrich Friedrich Karl Freiherr von Stein, a volatile and passionate advocate of change. Stein emerged from his first audience with the king charged with the invigoration of the nation and its preparation for a renewal of the struggle with Napoleon. The emancipation of the peasantry began in October and the reform of local government followed the next year. Simultaneously, the king set up a military reorganization commission to investigate the causes of the defeat and to propose changes in the army. Scharnhorst was the commission's president. Although temperamentally very different from Stein, and seen by many of his contemporaries as a pedant rather than a firebrand, Scharnhorst's conception of his task dovetailed with that of the civilian reformers. An army of free men which united the military and the nation would fight out of a sense of honour and patriotism.

Clausewitz asked Scharnhorst for a job as soon as he got back from France, but throughout 1808 he remained in the employ of Prince August. Scharnhorst none the less used Clausewitz to help with his literary production, the writing of patriotic pieces as well as the drafting of new regulations and articles for the press. Military reform, Clausewitz wrote anonymously in the *Jenaische Allgemeine Literatur-Zeitung*, rested 'on a new concept of the nation, a changed social consciousness, new economic thinking, and an altered relationship to policy – both in its assumptions and in its objectives'.[28] In January 1809 Clausewitz was placed at Scharnhorst's disposal in the Allgemeine Kriegsdepartement of the war ministry. When in June 1810 French pressure led to Scharnhorst's removal to the apparent backwater of the general staff, Clausewitz followed him. By now Clausewitz was effectively running Scharnhorst's office. Unlike Scharnhorst, Clausewitz did not have a decisive role in the military reform of Prussia, but the work on which he was engaged was both important and deeply practical. Clausewitz's reputation is as a theoretical and speculative thinker, but his service correspondence for the years 1809–12 is concerned with the minutiae of weapons production, with artillery and muskets, with what in *On War* he would see as the material issues ancillary to the art of war, not the art of war itself – a distinction which he made in 1811.[29]

The opportunity to reflect further on tactics arose in 1810, when Clausewitz became a professor at the Allgemeine Kriegsschule, successor to various military schools and forerunner of the Kriegsakademie, and was also given responsibility for teaching the Crown Prince, the future Friedrich Wilhelm IV. Clausewitz learnt to enjoy his pedagogic duties, although he undertook them with some reluctance, a point which underlined his burning desire to act rather than study. He and his colleagues watched the success of Spanish resistance to the French in 1808; they admired the performance of the Austrians in 1809, when Archduke Charles fought Napoleon to a standstill at Aspern-Essling; and they commented on the wisdom of Wellington's decision to withdraw to the lines of Torres Vedras around Lisbon in 1810. Clausewitz's focus remained fixed on readying Prussia for the renewal of the struggle with the French. Writing to Marie from Königsberg on 23 April 1809, he expressed his contempt for those 'who declare their loyalty to the king which prevents them detaching themselves from their pay and secure positions, who trumpet their patriotism which gives them a love of parades rather than battle, who constantly have the name of Prussia on their lips so as to avoid the name of Germany with its heavier and holier obligations'.[30]

Clausewitz was not as isolated as his frustration and self-pity sometimes suggested. In particular, in the autumn of 1808 he established a fresh and enduring friendship with August Wilhelm Neidhart von Gneisenau, the one true hero to emerge from the war of 1806. Gneisenau had led the defence of Kolberg until the peace of Tilsit, and was now a member of the military reform commission. Although Gneisenau, like Scharnhorst, was Clausewitz's senior in rank and age, the latter was soon writing in terms of apparent equality and warmth, moaning about his piles and exchanging family news. What really united the two of them, however, were their schemes for a war of national liberation.

Clausewitz had used the enforced idleness of the winter of 1808–9 to draft a memorandum on future operations in a war between Prussia and France. Much of this was a review of resources and possible allies, but at its heart were a clutch of ideas that would be developed and refined in the years up until 1812, and which reveal a more emotional, visceral and existential attitude to war than that embraced by the military thinkers of the eighteenth century or even by Clausewitz in his post-war writings, pre-eminently *On War*. Clausewitz rejected calculation and probability, since war brought chance and moral forces into play and so created its own possibilities. 'The series of consequences which follow from action are endless and the final result is therefore not accessible to human reason.' The justification for going to war rested less on its probable outcome than the cause which was at stake, and 'there is no more important aim than the independence of the state and nation'. Indeed, so vital was it that it warranted the greatest dangers. Lack of means therefore did not absolve Prussia or indeed all Germany from the obligation to recover their independence. The central task of the art of war was to fulfil this end by adapting the means available, a seemingly unexceptionable premise which led Clausewitz to a conclusion that could only be radical and shocking to those conditioned in the ways of the eighteenth century, and accustomed to defining the nation in terms of geography rather than of ideology or values: 'My idea is that it is necessary to sacrifice entirely a state that one can no longer defend so as to rescue the army.' The army should be freed from its obligation to defend the nation's territory, so that it would be able to follow purely military imperatives, using mobility and surprise, attacking the invader and – if need be – carrying on the war from outside the nation's frontiers. 'If therefore the Prussian army is not able to be linked to the state without perishing with it, if the downfall of the state is unavoidable, it seems to me that one can oppose the army to the state and affirm that it is wiser to trust the rights of the monarch to the former than to link them to the latter.'[31]

At one level, Clausewitz's belief that the army, not the state or even the king, could be the embodiment of the nation grew directly from the nature of the Prussia into which he had been born. But Frederick the Great had never imagined the possible separation of the three elements, not least because, threatened with Prussia's obliteration, he and the army had stood together. Clausewitz knew that in his own day the king and at least some of his officers were not so united. He dreaded being forced into a decision to fight against his own country because the king continued to kow-tow to France. Inspired by the Spanish example of national resistance and by similar news from Tyrol, Scharnhorst and Clausewitz drew up plans for a militia which would unite people and army in insurrection. In 1809 Gneisenau picked up on the idea that the war could be continued outside the nation's frontiers, planning the formation of a Prussian legion which would be paid for by Britain but would fight alongside Austria. Although French pressure on the king forced Gneisenau out of the army and into diplomacy, he continued to prepare for war against Napoleon, touring the capitals of Europe to drum up support. In 1811 Gneisenau drew up a scheme for a popular insurrection to which Clausewitz contributed by a study of a possible campaign in Silesia. Clausewitz wrote to Gneisenau in January 1811, anticipating Prussia's total defeat, but hoping that, if his country went down with honour, he too would go down with honour, 'or at least would sacrifice my own life'.[32]

On 24 February 1812, the moment which Scharnhorst,

Gneisenau and Clausewitz had so dreaded arrived. The renewal of hostilities between France and Russia loomed and the king again bent to French pressure. Unwilling to be the first to fight, and unsure how Russia and Austria would react, he agreed to Prussia's occupation by the French army and to provide 20,000 soldiers if war did break out between France and Russia. Scharnhorst tried to resign but was sent on leave. Clausewitz, who had run over his possible responses to this crisis many times, and who had considered joining the Austrian army in 1809, decided to leave the service of Prussia and join the Russian army. He was not alone, and, in response to a request from a group of like-minded officers, he drafted three political manifestos which he sent to Gneisenau. In the event they were not published until 1869, after they had been discovered in Gneisenau's papers.

The 1812 manifestos are the culmination of the thoughts first developed in the winter of 1807–8, and reveal Clausewitz at his most radical. The first manifesto reached its climax with a creed:

> I believe and confess that a people can value nothing more highly than the dignity and liberty of its existence.
>
> That it must defend these to the last drop of its blood.
>
> That there is no higher duty to fulfil, no higher law to obey.
>
> That the shameful blot of cowardly submission can never be erased.

> That this drop of poison in the blood of the nation is passed on to posterity, crippling and eroding the strength of future generations.
>
> That the honour of the king and government are one with the honour of the people, and the sole safeguard of its well-being.
>
> That a people courageously struggling for liberty is invincible.
>
> That even the destruction of liberty after a bloody and honourable struggle assures the people's rebirth. It is the seed of life, which one day will bring forth a new, securely rooted tree.[33]

For Clausewitz in 1812, therefore, war had its own purpose, and it was one which could be fulfilled even if it ended – as he expected it would – in defeat. As in 1806, he refused to see the outcome of any campaign as final. By the very act of resistance the nation would define itself. This was the Clausewitz cited by Hitler in *Mein Kampf*, not the author of *On War*.[34] His existential view of war assured his place in the Nazi pantheon, especially in the last days of the Third Reich, but finds only a very pale reflection in modern commentaries on Clausewitz's thinking. None the less, in *On War*, Book 6, chapter 26, Clausewitz rekindled his own responses of 1812 when he reminded governments fighting for their existence that they should never assume that their fate depends on a single decisive battle: 'There will always be time enough to die; like a drowning man who will clutch instinctively at a straw, it is the natural law of the moral world that a nation that finds itself on the brink of the abyss will try to save itself by any means.' And he concluded with words that hallowed the very act of fighting itself: 'No matter how small and weak a state may be in comparison with its enemy, it must not forego these last efforts, or one would conclude that its soul is dead.'[35]

Twenty years after the outbreak of the French revolutionary wars, such reflections on war itself should not have been too shocking in themselves: the peoples of Spain, Italy and Switzerland were putting them into practice. Far more sensitive, and far more damaging to Clausewitz's career, was what the manifestos said about kingship. Clausewitz prefaced the first manifesto with a quotation from Frederick the Great, and concluded the third in the same manner, but sandwiched between these appeals to Prussian tradition were sentiments to which Frederick had paid lip-service but which he had rarely shown signs of believing. 'The king is the representative of the nation', Clausewitz declared in the second manifesto. He went on to argue that the king and the nation had to stand together in defending their freedom against an implacable enemy. 'The king who perishes shamefully insults the nation and is the cause of its misfortune; the king who succumbs gloriously elevates the nation and his glorious name is balm on its wounds.'[36]

In Clausewitz's view the king's advisers had created a conflict of interest between the monarchy and the nation. Scharnhorst and Gneisenau felt similarly but managed to side-step the full implications of their beliefs. By exchanging the blue coat of Prussia for the green of Russia, Clausewitz went one stage further, rupturing his connections with the court, and confronting the possible seizure of his property. He felt bitter and isolated, his professional ambition the victim of a tension between his patriotism and the Prussian monarchy, and was now cast into a world he did not know in an army whose language he could not speak. He wrote to Marie in August 1812, complaining of the rigours of the Russian retreat across a devastated landscape, of the heat and dust, and of the lack of food and water. He was only thirty-two, but he was suffering from gout and toothache; his hair had begun to fall out and his hands looked like yellow leather.

In 1804 Clausewitz had predicted that, if Napoleon invaded Russia, he would be defeated,[37] but in all his writings on the 1812 campaign Clausewitz refused to criticize Napoleon's strategy. 'Bonaparte wanted to conduct and conclude the war in Russia as he had conducted and concluded all his campaigns. To begin with decisive blows and to employ the advantages he gained from them to achieve further decisive battles, always placing his winnings on the next card until the bank was broken – *that was his way*, and it must be said that he owed the tremendous success that he had achieved only to *this way*; his degree of success was scarcely conceivable by any other means.'[38] What broke the French army was not, Clausewitz stressed, the retreat from Moscow, but the advance, not the sufferings of the winter but the privations of the summer. Again Napoleon had little option. His goal was 'to beat the enemy – to shatter him – to gain the capital – to drive the government into the last corner of the empire – and then, while the confusion was fresh, to dictate the peace'.[39] This too was what had worked in the past. He had broken the shackles of eighteenth-century warfare by using requisition as his principal means of supply rather than relying too much on magazines to his rear. As a result he had achieved speed and range in his campaigns. He could not have abandoned the system of requisitioning for the Russian campaign, although Clausewitz did acknowledge that he might have invaded on a broader front so as to spread the effects of his army's depredations. The wear and tear of his advance meant that Napoleon fought the battle of Borodino with an army equal in size – not superior – to the Russians, and reached Moscow with only 90,000 men, not 200,000. No more than one third of the French losses in the advance were due to fighting.[40]

Several observers in Prussia, Scharnhorst and Gneisenau among them, had realized that a retreat into the interior was Russia's best chance of victory. Although Clausewitz probably also favoured this approach, it does not follow that he thought it would be successful. In May 1812 he was appointed to the staff of Karl Ludwig von Phull, who had taught him at the war school and who had joined the Russian army after 1806. Phull was the victim of not one but two of Clausewitz's devastating pen portraits, one each for 1806 and 1812, a man who was deemed by others to be intelligent but who in Clausewitz's view lacked a grasp of reality. Phull advised the Tsar to retreat but not sufficiently far to take the army out of range of Napoleon's initial blows and so to achieve the effects that the retreat in fact accomplished. 'The campaign,' Clausewitz later wrote, 'worked out its own form, and Phull's idea has the less pretension to be considered the leading one, as in itself it was a false one.'[41] Clausewitz managed to extricate himself from Phull's employment, and was attached as a staff officer to a cavalry corps which formed part of the Russian rearguard. He was present at the actions of Vitebsk and Smolensk as well as at Borodino.

In early November, as the French retreated back along the route by which they had come (as Clausewitz again sagely pointed out, Napoleon had little choice as that was where his magazines were), Clausewitz realized that he had fought in a campaign which was among 'the most original in military history' and perhaps 'the richest in its consequences for the history of states'.[42] Joining the army of Ludwig Adolf Peter von Wittgenstein, he witnessed the final horrors of the French attempt to pull the remnants of the Grande Armée across the Beresina. Speared by Cossacks or frozen in the river's icy waters, 30,000 stragglers succumbed. 'If my feelings had not already been hardened or rather blunted, the horror and shock would have driven me out of my mind, and as it is I shall not be able to think of it for many years without terror.'[43]

Within a month, however, Clausewitz's reactions turned to joy. On 25 December in Kurland, Hans von Yorck, commanding the Prussian contingent with the French army, found himself cut off by Wittgenstein's advance from the main French formations on Napoleon's northern flank, and entered negotiations with the pursuing Russians. Clausewitz himself became the emissary between the two sides and on 30 December 1812 a convention was concluded at Tauroggen which declared the Prussian corps to be neutral. Clausewitz was no longer alone – and in two senses. First was the elation of hearing his own language and seeing familiar faces. Second was the knowledge that his political isolation was drawing to a close. Yorck was seen as a conservative officer, but now he too had put nation before king. Stein, removed from office in 1808 thanks to French pressure and also exiled to Russia, promptly convened an assembly in East Prussia and persuaded it to mobilize all able-bodied men of military age for the purposes of self-defence against the French. The king was dragged along by the pressure of events. In February 1813 Prussia finally adopted universal conscription and in March applied the East Prussian model in the creation of a militia or Landwehr. Army, nation and monarchy had been united through radical, if not revolutionary, reform, and it was the army which had carried it into effect.

On 16 March 1813 the king declared war on Napoleon. The so-called war of national liberation was even more important in the telling than it was in reality. Thanks to pressure from Gneisenau, Clausewitz was one of its earliest propagandists, rushing a small book, *Der Feldzug von 1813 bis zum Waffenstillstand*, into print in the same year. Prefaced with remarks about slaves throwing off the yoke of tyranny, it took its story back to 1806, and not unreasonably concluded with Clausewitz's own amazement at the rapidity of the French collapse. In December 1812 the Russian army was as depleted and exhausted as that of France, and Clausewitz had feared that the kings of Prussia and Austria would continue to sit on the fence, with the result that Europe would still be at war ten years hence.[44] But Tauroggen meant that Prussia had picked up the baton just as Russia faltered, and Napoleon was therefore still on the ropes in the summer of 1813. 'Who, if he had been told that in six months the Emperor Napoleon would have several hundred thousand more men in Germany, and that he would commit himself to two major battles with superior numbers, would not have believed that the allies would have fallen apart and become disheartened, retreated deep back into Poland and Prussia, and that the consequence would have been the silencing of Austria?'[45]

There was bickering between Russia and Prussia; Napoleon did manage to raise a fresh army with phenomenal speed, and in his advance towards Leipzig and Dresden won hard-fought victories at Lützen on 2 May 1813 and Bautzen on 20–21 May. But in the armistice which followed, the Prussian and Russian armies completed their recovery and Austria committed itself to the alliance against France. As Wellington advanced into southern France, the three continental allies combined to defeat Napoleon at Leipzig in a battle which showed how much warfare had changed within the short span of Clausewitz's military career. At Valmy in 1792, the first victory of France's revolutionary army and, in Goethe's words, 'a new epoch in the history of the world', 64,000 men confronted at most 30,000 and the battle lasted a single day. At Leipzig, the allies fielded 365,000 men to Napoleon's 195,000 in a battle which extended over three days, from 16 October to 19 October.[46] The emperor was defeated, lost control east of the Rhine, and fell back to France. He sought terms in April 1814.

Clausewitz had been careful to stress in his booklet that 'the king and his ministers had understood the mood of the nation and shared its feelings'.[47] But in practice Friedrich Wilhelm could not forgive and forget. Throughout 1813, Clausewitz soldiered on as a Russian officer, even though at first he did so in Blücher's headquarters. At Lützen, concluding that all possibilities of effective command had gone, he had rushed into the mêlée, sword in hand, and received a French bayonet thrust behind his ear. Scharnhorst suffered a wound to his leg, which was at first not deemed to be dangerous, but he died in Prague on 28 June. Clausewitz was distraught: 'Although he is irreplaceable to the army, the state and Europe, I can scarcely think of these considerations; only that I lose at this moment the dearest friend of my life [and this to his devoted wife], whom I can never replace with another, and whom I shall always miss.'[48]

Once again, therefore, joy was sullied. Scharnhorst's death made Gneisenau his principal protector and the latter asked for Clausewitz's services when he was apointed Governor-General of Silesia as well as Chief of Staff to Blücher. The king refused Gneisenau's request. In late 1812 the Russians had begun the formation of a German legion of their own, and it was to this that Clausewitz now turned, becoming its Chief of Staff just as hostilities were renewed after the armistice of 1813. Thus he was not present at the battle of Leipzig and his advance on France ran by way of north Germany, Denmark and the Low Countries. Although Clausewitz's corps fought a couple of significant actions, this was a war principally of skirmishes and outposts, of diversion and harassment: small war in the parlance of the day. Its purpose was to tie down French forces and so prevent their use in the main theatre of operations. When Clausewitz finally entered the country of the arch-fiend in 1814 he did not fight his way in, nor – unlike his entry in 1807 – did he come as a captive. He was surprised by how pleasant he found it, although he was not impressed by French cuisine: 'what should be sweet was sour,' he told Marie, 'and what should be neither was both at the same time'.[49]

On 11 April 1814 Clausewitz was recommissioned in the Prussian army in the rank of colonel and the German legion was taken into Prussian service. His body was suffering the effects of his campaigns, and he relieved the pain with opium or by taking the waters at a spa. But his active soldiering was not quite done. In March 1815, when Napoleon escaped from Elba, Clausewitz secured an appointment as Chief of Staff to one of the four corps that Prussia put into the field under Blücher's command. On 15 June Napoleon advanced into Belgium and on the following day hit the Prussians at Ligny before they were fully concentrated. Clausewitz's corps, commanded by Johann Adolph von Thielmann, was criticized for its caution, its principal role being to cover the Prussian line of retreat to the east. But when the Prussians did fall back, Gneisenau, the Chief of Staff to Blücher, who had been incapacitated by a fall from his horse, broke with orthodoxy. He abandoned the Prussian line of communications, moving northwest and so closer to Wellington's army, itself engaged with a French force on the same day at Quatre Bras. As a result the allied forces were able to converge on the field of Waterloo (or Belle Alliance as Clausewitz called it) on 18 June. Thielmann's corps was not engaged at Waterloo, but was fighting a bitter defensive action at Wavre, so preventing the French corps under Marquis Emmanuel de Grouchy from rejoining Napoleon's main body. As morning broke on 19 June, Wellington and Blücher pressed their advance, but Thielmann and Clausewitz retreated.

Clausewitz was once again peripheral to the main story. Moreover, when he had had opportunities for decisive action, albeit fleeting ones, he had seemed to fumble them. He would not now exercise a major command in the field. Nor had he any wish to re-engage with Prussian politics. He was disenchanted by Prussia's vengeful behaviour in Paris, urging moderation and remarking how much more effective were the coolness and integrity of the British. He was put forward as a possible ambassador to London in 1821, but he was deemed to be too brusque, too undiplomatic, and – above all – too radical for such a post.

Domestic politics proved as abhorrent and tricky. With the war over, the king and his advisers moved to limit the effect of their own actions of 1813. Part of the myth of the war of national liberation was that it represented a genuine outpouring of voluntary patriotic sentiment. In reality the volunteers were small in number and militarily ineffective. Clausewitz criticized the so-called Freikorps for their divisive effects, for taking away the social leaders who should have been the core of the Landwehr. Compulsory service in the latter, not voluntary enlistment in the former, enabled Prussia to raise 300,000 men by August 1813. In his view the proof of the pudding was in the eating: Prussia was a military loser before 1813, a victor thereafter.

Clausewitz's concerns over the future of the Landwehr were primarily military. The Napoleonic wars had taught him that numbers were normally decisive: Prussia was still a small state in a Europe of bigger ones, and it needed to be able to maximize its manpower. This was a matter of self-defence, 'of existence or non-existence'. The whole population needed to acquire 'a martial spirit and institutions'.[50] But as reactionary forces regained their foothold after 1815, the Landwehr's political aspects seemed to be more significant than its military utility. A military force that was organized locally, that put arms in the hands of the entire male population of military age, could lead the mob to decide that it was the nation, and so become a tool of revolution, of domestic chaos, not of external security. This was a risk Clausewitz was prepared to take, preferring the risk of revolution, which Prussia had not in fact suffered and, if it were to eventuate, would come whether or not there was a Landwehr, to 'the danger of invasion and enslavement', about which Prussia had learnt all too much in recent years.[51] The principle of the Landwehr survived the reaction but the practice was cut back. Clausewitz argued that the Landwehr was superior to the regular army. In fact it was subordinated to the standing army, its local roots were cut and its political influence curtailed.

Despite his distance from the court and his lack of patrons, Clausewitz, who had been Chief of Staff to the Prussian troops based on Koblenz since 1815, was promoted to major-general when the allies met for the congress of Aix-la-Chapelle in September 1818. Once the congress had completed its deliberations, he was free to take up the post to which he had been appointed in May 1818, that of director of the Allgemeine Kriegsschule in Berlin. His tasks were solely administrative. He did not teach, but he did have plenty of time for his own studies and access to an excellent library, and he could socialize in the company of savants as well as soldiers. He became less angry and more reflective, less of a German nationalist and more of a Prussian liberal. Perhaps most importantly for the creative process he and Marie were no longer separated by social convention or wartime service: most of his writing was done in her room, not in his study.

Clausewitz had turned his back on politics, but it had not turned its back on him. In 1830, just after revolution had toppled the Bourbons in France and with the threat of it elsewhere, Clausewitz was appointed inspector of artillery in Breslau. In December revolution threw the Russians out of Poland, and the king feared that disturbances could cross the frontier into Prussia. He formed an army of observation, which he placed under Gneisenau's command. The old warrior asked for Clausewitz as his Chief of Staff. Clausewitz's pessimism, combined with his restless, probing mind, led him to anticipate not just widespread revolution but also its concomitant, European war, writing to Gneisenau on 13 November 1830 that war would be unavoidable in the new year.[52] To the west there was the possibility of French intervention in Belgium and to the east Russia was struggling to regain control of Poland. Prussia declared itself to be neutral, neither directly helping its wartime ally in Poland nor squashing the French. Clausewitz feared that small fissures in the alliance of 1813–15 could quickly become major divisions. 'All these things, when I think of them, fill me with unspeakable sadness,' he wrote to Marie on 9 June 1831, 'and leave me with no other consolation than the fact that we, the two of us, have only a small part of our lives in front of us, and that we leave no children behind us.'[53] On 23 August Gneisenau succumbed to cholera with Clausewitz by his side. Clausewitz's depression took a further dive downwards. The responses to the reports he sent back from Posen (today's Poznan) to Friedrich Wilhelm III – or the lack of them – he saw as renewed evidence of royal disdain. He returned to Breslau to be reunited with Marie on 9 November. On the afternoon of 16 November he showed the first signs of cholera, and died that night, probably of a heart attack. To his doctors and to Marie, his general medical condition, the aches and pains which had dogged him throughout the 1820s, were more responsible for his death than the epidemic which was sweeping central Europe.

It seemed as though he had been a comparatively minor player in some of the greatest events of the world. It appeared too that his career, which he believed could so easily have flourished if he and his king had been minded to pursue similar rather than divergent courses, always stuttered rather than burst into flame. In fact the decade of apparent inactivity at the war school in Berlin enabled him to achieve something far more lasting – to reflect on the range and diversity of war which he had encountered in the previous two.

CHAPTER 2

The Writing of *On War*

'Meanwhile I am even more, and principally, on my own and that enables me to get on with writing the description I have begun of war,' Clausewitz wrote to Gneisenau from Koblenz on 14 November 1816.[1] Marie confirmed that 1816 was the year in which her husband began to harvest what she called 'the fruit that had ripened in the course of his rich experiences during four significant years of warfare'.[2] But her statement reveals more than the centrality of the Russian campaign and the war of national liberation to Clausewitz's ideas about war. It refers to the fact that in early 1812, just before he left for Russia, Clausewitz completed a short manuscript on 'the most important principles for the conduct of war' for his pupil, the Crown Prince.

In other words Clausewitz began to put pen to paper on the theory of war before he declared his intention to write a major book on the subject. The issue of the origins of *On War* are therefore more vexed than its author's simple declaration of 1816 suggests. Marie herself referred to the decisive influence of Scharnhorst, which Clausewitz first felt almost a decade earlier and which found its reflection in some thoughts on strategy dated to 1804. Peter Paret therefore argues that 'from the outset [Clausewitz] travelled a straight road', even contending that it was the campaigns of 1793–4 which set him on the 'path of recognizing war as a political phenomenon'.[3]

Paret's argument that there is a fundamental consistency to Clausewitz's thought – if justified – is of basic importance to a reading of *On War*. The book was not finished when Clausewitz went off to Breslau in 1830 and it was left to a distraught Marie to put his papers in order and publish them, with the assistance of her brother Friedrich Wilhelm von Brühl, himself a lieutenant-general, and of Major Franz August O'Etzel, who had taught at the war school under Clausewitz and took charge of the maps. The first three volumes of Clausewitz's *Hinterlassene Werke* covered *On War* and appeared between 1832 and 1834; the last and tenth was published in 1837, a year after Marie's own death.

This first edition of *On War* contained basic misprints as well as more fundamental contradictions and obscurities. There are references to chapters that are not present, and to topics which Clausewitz says he will treat in one chapter and in fact appear in another. Clausewitz promised a ninth book, on 'absolute war', of which we have nothing.[4] Despite the books' poor sales, a new edition, prepared by Friedrich von Brühl, appeared between 1853 and 1857. Brühl made necessary corrections but also altered more fundamentally the paragraph on the position of the

Commander-in-Chief in the Cabinet, contained in Book 8, chapter 6B. Brühl's version, unlike that in the first edition, suggested that the Commander-in-Chief should take part in all the Cabinet's decisions, not just those concerning war. It could therefore be construed as advocating military intervention in politics. Given Clausewitz's actions in 1812, the wording of the second edition was not unreasonable, but, to those considering Clausewitz's legacy in the light of Germany's role in two world wars, the corruption of the text made him a father of German militarism.

The significance of this change is perhaps less important than others made by Brühl and O'Etzel, which unlike this one we cannot now trace because they were made to the first edition. The first volume of the *Hinterlassene Werke*, embracing Books 1, 2, 3 and 4 of *On War*, was prefaced by an introduction by Marie. She explained that her brother had found a note written by Clausewitz on 10 July 1827, in which he regarded the first six books as in a complete form but all of which needed revising, and that he intended to begin the process when he had finished Books 7 and 8. Marie went on to say that, in the light of this note, her brother had inserted the revisions 'in those parts of Book 1 for which they were intended'.[5] Marie wrote another introduction to the third volume, which included Books 7 and 8 of *On War*, those on the attack and on war planning respectively. Both were described as sketches in the original German edition, and Marie thanked O'Etzel for putting them in order. Brühl's and O'Etzel's interventions therefore potentially covered all of Books 1 and 8, the two seen today as the most important and relevant of *On War*, but we now have no way of knowing their extent. Much has to be inferred from the note written by Clausewitz in 1827, which Marie cited, and which is published as an Introduction to every edition of *On War*, and to a further note which was unfinished and undated, in which he says that he regarded only Book 1, chapter 1, as finished but 'will at least serve the whole by indicating the direction I meant to follow everywhere'.[6]

Peter Paret and Michael Howard presumed that this second note was written in 1830 as Clausewitz left for Breslau. If they are right, we seem to confront a stark, if superficial choice: either only Book 1, chapter 1, is worth serious attention, or (as Paret and Howard have in fact argued) the entire text of *On War* matters because it represents an evolutionary flow of which Book 1, chapter 1, is only the essence. But Werner Hahlweg dated this note to 1827, and with good reason. The note describes a text concerned only with a single sort of war, 'major war' of the type fought by Napoleon, and whose analysis dominated Books 3 to 5 (a point glossed over by Howard and Paret through the omission in their translation of the reference to 'major war'). In other words, when he wrote this note, Clausewitz had not yet acknowledged the need for a theory that embraced other forms of war or fully incorporated the dialectical method which would allow him to do that to such effect in Books 6 to 8, as well as in Books 1 and

2. If the second note is dated to 1827, Clausewitz had the time to revise much more than just Book 1, let alone only its first chapter, and there are indications that he did so. Book 2, chapters 2 and 3, are, like Book 1, chapter 1, organized in a logical sequence, with step-by-step numbered paragraphs, and their argument relates both to Book 1 and to the introductory first chapter of Book 8. Clausewitz saw Book 8 as dealing with the 'direction of the whole war' and planned to use it, not Book 1, to make clear the sweep of his ideas, a point confirmed in the unfinished note.[7] Marie appended to the published version of Book 8 the title 'sketch', but it is not a sketch in the same sense as Book 7, which was similarly described. It is much fuller and more developed, suggesting that serious work was done on it after the undated note was penned. Its last chapter moves from the abstract to the harshly concrete, concluding with a plan for a coalition war with France. Designed to bring France 'to her knees' and to teach her 'a lesson any time she chooses to resume her insolent behaviour with which she has burdened Europe for a hundred and fifty years', the plan reflects not just the central preoccupation of Clausewitz's active military career but also that of the last months of his life.[8] It could therefore be argued that he had last revisited Book 8 in 1830 itself.

The note that is dated to 1827 provides indirect corroboration for this approach, as it introduces ideas wholly absent from the undated note, suggesting that the latter was written not only before 1830 but also before 10 July

1827. In the dated note Clausewitz suggests possible solutions to the dilemmas posed by the undated note. He argues that there are two types of war, not one: war designed to destroy the enemy politically or militarily, and war designed to occupy some portion of the enemy's territory. In the first case the victor can dictate the peace; in the second the terms of the peace will be negotiated. Clausewitz then went on to say that 'apart from this difference existing in fact between wars, we must further expressly and exactly establish the point of view, no less necessary in practice, from which war is regarded as nothing but the continuation of state policy with other means'. He did not at this stage say specifically that this third proposition was what gave unity to the first two, although that is an easy and logical connection. This point was to be fully applied in Book 8, and only when he had done that would he be ready to develop the idea in Book 1 and then go on to revise Books 2 to 6 with this consideration in mind. The implication of Clausewitz's dated note, therefore, is that as of July 1827 Books 2 to 6 had not been revised and were as a result in some senses at odds with Books 1 and 8. Clausewitz himself concluded: 'Should I be interrupted in this work by an untimely death, what exists of it may certainly be described as merely a hotchpotch of ideas, which being exposed to ceaseless misunderstandings, will give rise to a multitude of ceaseless criticisms.'[9]

The depressed tone may be a consequence of the serious illness which Clausewitz suffered in 1827. The note was unnecessarily self-deprecatory (not a characteristic he often displayed and one immediately contradicted by his claim at the end of the note that his book, even in its incomplete state, might revolutionize the theory of war). In 1804, in a paragraph on the planning of operations, Clausewitz had made exactly the same distinction between the two types of war that he made in his note of 1827. But he did not develop the point, and he saw no necessary connection between the political objectives in war and the manner of its conduct. The former were of two sorts, the latter was of one. 'In both cases', he continued, 'the intention must be to cripple the enemy's forces, so that he either cannot, or cannot without danger to his existence, carry on the war.' The greatest commanders had always set out to destroy the enemy's army, and in this respect doing anything other than seeking the most decisive operations with the maximum effort was being 'penny wise but pound foolish'.[10]

In 1804 Napoleon was honing the Grande Armée; he had yet to apply it on the battlefield. The central difficulty with Paret's argument for an intellectual continuity in Clausewitz's writings between 1804 and 1830 is Clausewitz's own emphasis on experience. What happened after 1804, and up to 1815, was fundamental to the writing of *On War*. The French Revolution may have inaugurated massive changes in the way in which war was conducted but neither their true cause nor their full implications were necessarily evident to their opponents. It was Napoleon who perfected these innovations and made them into method, so that for the first time – as Clausewitz saw it – wars between civilized states were fought beyond the point where the defeated side could maintain itself. The Prussian conduct of war, inherited from the eighteenth century and adapted for wars with lesser objectives, simply did not work in wars of national survival. At Jena in 1806 Prussia confronted 'the God of War himself'.[11]

The war which the adult Clausewitz experienced involved armies often three times the size of those of his youth, committed to a strategy of overthrow, and in which nationalism was the key component of full mobilization. Throughout the years after 1816 Clausewitz was digesting that experience. The change of pace to his own life was itself important: the man of action, the deeply politicized soldier, living with passion at the centre of major events, became an academic, deliberative and more detached. He was also older. The Clausewitz of 1827 was a different man from the Clausewitz of 1812. Because it was his wont to return to his writings, revising them and rethinking them, and often treating the same topic more than once, it can be difficult to establish when he wrote what. His account of the defeat of 1806, *Nachrichten über Preussen in seiner grossen Katastrophe*, not included by his widow in the collected works, was probably first completed in 1823–4, but originated in his published letters of 1807 and was revised in 1828. He took up the story of the Napoleonic wars in earnest with his account of the Russian campaign of 1812, completed after 1824 according to Paret, and covered each of 1813, 1814 and

1815 in separate works: that on 1813 very soon after the events, that on 1814 – the most sustained attempt to use a campaign for strategic analysis in a didactic fashion – very soon after the peace, and that on Waterloo shortly before his death.[12] In addition, in the second half of the 1820s he wrote histories of two earlier campaigns in which he himself had not personally served – that of Napoleon in Italy 1796, and that in Italy and Switzerland in 1799, the last being the longest and most developed of all his histories.

This was an enormous output, and it was sustained alongside his theoretical work. Nor is it separate from it. 'We want above all to make clear the unclear assumptions which we encounter in the conduct of major war,' he wrote in his history of the 1799 campaign, in order to justify a digression on army organization.[13] Scharnhorst, after all, had taught him that military history should be the basis for theory, and in 1812 he passed that view on to the Crown Prince, as it 'makes us see things as they are and as they function'.[14] Each of the principal milestones in Clausewitz's active military career taught him something different about the nature of war. Jena showed him that war could effect revolutionary change, albeit not as an end in itself but as a means to mobilize the nation for war. It installed Napoleon as the model for how war could be conducted, but then the Russian campaign revealed that even he had limitations, that delaying battle – not seeking it, as Napoleon did – could be a strategy for the defence. It also opened out the possibility of the role of policy in shaping war, an approach which blossomed in 1815, when Napoleon was finally defeated not just on the battlefield but by an alliance which was able to compose its differences, to coordinate its actions and to apply them to achieve an enduring peace.[15]

This is not to suggest that, as Clausewitz became aware of each fresh dimension, he ditched the old: his great strength was his increasing awareness of the diversity of war. But this deep historical study did confront him with a fundamental problem, that the late Napoleonic wars – which were the basis of his own experience, and therefore the template for much that he wrote in Books 3 to 5 of *On War* – did not match all the wars that had been fought in the past, or might be fought in the future. Since his ambition was to establish something that explained war as a universal phenomenon, the undated note and the note of 1827 mark a crisis in Clausewitz's thinking: a moment when he realized that as well as being rooted in his own experience he had to rise above it. The acknowledgement that there were two different types of war was at odds with the thrust of what he had written thus far, which described war as a unitary phenomenon. Moreover, although the note of 1827 was unequivocal in its assertion that war was the continuation of state policy, Clausewitz presented that as another, independent insight. It was not yet a way out of an otherwise insoluble dilemma – how to write about the theory of war and at the same time embrace the diversity of its forms. He would only realize that as he worked through the implications of his own thinking.[16]

He clearly did this quickly, no doubt in part because of the enormous body of work that he had already done, stretching back to 1804 and possibly before. Barely five months after composing the note of 10 July 1827, on 22 December Clausewitz wrote a long reply to a letter from Major Carl Ferdinand von Roeder, an officer on the General Staff, who had asked Clausewitz for his views on his solutions to the problems of a defensive war for Prussia. Clausewitz reflected the point of his July note when he said that people had begun to assume that 'the plans and actions' created by the circumstances of the French Revolution and Napoleon 'were universal norms'. He went on: 'Such a view would summarily reject the entire history of war, which is absurd.' The fact that war could be of two types must lead to the recognition that 'war is a political act which is not wholly autonomous; a true political instrument that does not act on its own but is controlled by something else, the hand of policy'. By December 1827, therefore, policy had become for Clausewitz the unifying theme for his theory of war.[17]

In July he had averred that the two approaches to going to war pervaded them and kept them apart; in December, policy pervaded all war, including its purely military elements, and therefore united the two in a single concept. Once again the path was open to a universal theory of war, but it would not be a theory based solely on the practice of late Napoleonic war. This is why Book 1, chapter 1, is different from so much else of *On War*: it represents a synthesis. The origins of Book 1 do indeed go back to 1804, which is when Clausewitz began writing about the theory of war. Many (but not all) of the ideas expressed then were the embryos from which more developed concepts would grow. But his approach was to write organically, constantly rethinking which chapters – which insights – belonged in which books, shuffling material between books, building up observations, but then striving to pare down his prose, so that the results were succinct and aphoristic. Moreover, the organization of material was not clearly mapped out from the beginning. The notes of 1804 do not have a clear sequence, and themes which have been covered before recur as though they are new items. He added to the edifice in 1807–12, and then began again in 1816. He had a clear sense of many major themes by 1818. The bulk of Books 2 to 6, which are overwhelmingly concerned with the practice of late Napoleonic warfare, were written between then and 1827, and reflect the fruit of Clausewitz's engagement with the histories of the wars which he had experienced. Book 6, that on the defence, represented the culmination of this stage of the process, and was possibly the progenitor of the crisis which the note of July 1827 represents. He observed that it had made him realize that the object of his work was not to provide new principles for the conduct of war, but 'the essential content of what has long existed'.[18]

Book 6 contrasts with Book 1: his preference, to present his ideas in 'compressed form, like small nuggets of compressed metal',[19] was achieved in the latter but not in the former. It is the least disciplined and by far the biggest of the books, representing about a quarter of the whole. Much of it is repetitious: some of its material could have been reallocated to earlier books, or is already covered in them. Its counterpoise – Book 7 on the attack – is by contrast the shortest and least developed book of *On War*, partly because there is in fact a great deal on the offensive in Book 6, and partly – presumably – because Clausewitz did not live long enough to think through the relationship between the two books in a more sustained way and so achieve a better balance. The writing of Book 6 raised two fundamental issues for Clausewitz. First, the discussion of defence comes at the intersection of the peculiarity of his own experience and his generalizations about war as a whole. His assertion of the inherent strength of the defence rests on a basic truth, validated by what he had seen in 1812, but it is propped up by the sort of value judgements, questionable as general principles, which he did not permit himself elsewhere. The reason was that Clausewitz's interest in the inherent strengths of the defence was driven less by abstract concerns regarding strategy than by his patriotic concern for Prussian policy after 1806. Prussia after Jena could no more behave as an aggressive state than could Frederick the Great in the later stages of the Seven Years War: the aim of both was survival. Here for the first time, therefore, he acknowledged the role of policy in permeating war. States, like Prussia in 1806 or Russia in 1812, could fight a politically defensive war: the manner in which it was waged might, however, be offensive or defensive, largely depending on the resources available to them.

Raymond Aron regarded Book 6, not Book 1 or Book 8, as the most important of *On War*, and he may well have been right, not least because it is on the cusp in the development of Clausewitz's thought. But Clausewitz did not return to it. Indeed, he could not think about doing so until he had completed its obverse, Book 7, on the attack, in the same detail. Instead, he produced only a sketch of that book, because – it would seem – he was anxious to get on with Book 8. His note of 10 July 1827, which makes clear that he felt like a man living on borrowed time, says that he regarded Book 8 as the clearing house for his ideas, and that he intended to write that before turning to the revision of Books 1 to 6. If the undated note was written in 1830, then the contradictions between Books 1 and 8 are explained by the evolution of his ideas over a three-year period, and Book 1, chapter 1, can claim to be 'superior' and more polished than Book 8. If it predates the July 1827 note, Book 8 has to be seen in a very different light. Then contradictions between Books 1 and 8 are not to be explained simply by the move from Book 8 back to Book 1, but by further work on Book 8 itself, which could have left it in some respects as more definitive than Book 1.[20]

The change which the note of July 1827 represents goes

even further than its implications for the order in which the books were written and what that says about the evolution of Clausewitz's ideas. It also marks a change of method. The two types of war which the note described were not real, but ideals, contrasting poles to make a dialectical point. Clausewitz was consistently vitriolic in his condemnation of those military writers who created systems of war, especially Bülow and Jomini. He took particular exception to those who interpreted as dogma rules derived from geography, mathematics and – as he put it – geology (by which he meant the determinants of terrain). 'They aim at fixed values; but in war everything is uncertain, and calculations have to be made with variable qualities.'[21] But his objection was not to systems in themselves but to systems based on false principles. Despite his protests to the contrary, *On War* says a great deal about geography, especially mountains, and not a little about geometry. All Clausewitz's introductory notes to *On War* testify to his own desire to systematize. Book 4, chapter 11, on the use of the battle, declares that 'a deliberately planned great battle… is more or less, but always in some degree, to be regarded as the leading means and central point of the whole system'. At the beginning of the next chapter, on the strategic means of exploiting victory, Clausewitz states that his intention is to find out how the battle 'is connected with the whole system of war'.[22] His quarrel was with systems which derived their core from a discipline alien to war's reality: if driven by geometry, for example, then they reached conclusions set by geometry, not rooted in war as he had experienced it. The purpose of Books 2 to 6 of *On War*, therefore, was to deal with war as it really was, precisely to develop sound principles. These books are distinguished less by debate than by the establishment of their own precepts: they are the ones which convey a unitary image of war. In Book 3 (on strategy), chapter 14, Clausewitz wrote: 'Soon the actor in war must simplify the law to some prominent characteristic points which form his rules, soon the method which he has adopted must become the staff on which he leans.'[23] Moreover, many of the principles which Clausewitz endorsed are to be found in Jomini as well.

Clausewitz magnified his differences with Jomini, Bülow and others for a purpose. He did not cite military writers of his own day with whom he agreed. Mention has already been made of Guibert. Equally noteworthy for their absence are the Germans, Georg Heinrich von Berenhorst, whose *Betrachtungen über den Kriegskunst* (1797) anticipated Clausewitz in several ways, not least in his emphasis on moral and psychological factors in war, and Johann Jakob Otto August Rühle von Lilienstern, Clausewitz's direct contemporary, who had stressed that war fulfilled political purposes in his war school lectures, published as a handbook for officers in 1817–18. Their omission may be due to vanity, to Clausewitz's own intellectual arrogance. But it also reflects their redundance in Clausewitz's scheme of things: his argument did not need them, even as buttresses for his more controversial assertions, but it did need Jomini and Bülow. They were the fall guys off whom he could bounce his propositions. Much of *On War* is a dialogue. In this Clausewitz is different from many other writers on strategy, not least Jomini, who tend to present conclusions rather than engage in argument and debate. But Clausewitz's predilection for the dialectical method is much less evident in Books 2 to 5, those in which he is describing late Napoleonic warfare and spelling out the principles to be derived from it, than it is in Books 1 and 8, those which have had a much more lasting influence on strategic thought.

Again, the completion of Book 6 marks the change in approach. Book 6, which stresses that the defence is the stronger form of war with the negative aim, is in tension with Book 7, the attack, which is the weaker form of war with the positive aim. Therefore, one of Clausewitz's central themes, that war is a reciprocal activity which depends on the clash of forces to occur at all, has become an analytical method. The big challenge that confronted him, as he embraced both the dialectic of attack and defence within war and the dialectic within his own book, was what that meant for his yen to find a system. The note of 1827 deepened the dilemma, with its statement that there were two sorts of wars. As the influence of dialectics became progressively stronger in Book 8, it confronted him with fresh challenges. One was the consequence of his own dialogue between theory and reality. It is not always clear from his writings when Clausewitz is establishing a normative principle as opposed to reflecting on experience. This is a natural outgrowth of his approach to principles, which he sees not as invariably true, but as generally true in the majority of cases – and that is precisely their value.

By December 1827 policy had become the basis for a new synthesis. Methodologically Clausewitz moved on from dialectics – from the Socratic mode of enquiry, which by leaving no assumption unchallenged was in danger of destroying more than creating – to a greater positivism. Throughout *On War*, Clausewitz displayed a propensity for seeing issues in threes. Many of these trios were prosaic. There were three reasons for having stronger vanguards in the centre, three conditions affecting the establishment of camps, three conditions under which armies could be quartered, three spatially distinct bases of operations, three effects of terrain on war, three types of pursuit, three strategic assets in controlling high ground, three factors which gave the decisive advantage in an engagement (surprise, the benefit of the terrain and concentric attack), and three advantages in mounting a converging attack.[24] So great was the drive to create groups of three, greater than logic alone suggested, that they could be the consequence of contrivance. Clausewitz said that there were three sorts of terrain different from plains; they were mountains, forests and marshes, and agricultural areas.[25] But what was the logic that lumped forests and marshes into a single category, when their impact on fighting could clearly be very different? And why were not plains themselves deemed to be a fourth type of terrain? In this case five categories were lurking under Clausewitz's rule of three.

Clausewitz's use of threes was repeated and frequent, although rarely as doggedly adhered to as in this case. It developed from being a device for enumerating issues on which he wished to comment, or distinctions which he wished to draw, to being a means for defining concepts central to his understanding of war. Victory was evident in three ways – in the enemy's loss of material strength, in the blow to his morale, and in his decision to abandon his intentions; the outcome of battle was measured by its psychological effect in the opposing general, the casualties that his army suffered, and the ground that he gave up; and its effects were therefore felt on the commanders, on the belligerent states, and on the course of the war.[26] What is evident here is that the groups of three combine to form a whole. Many of the pairs created by Clausewitz's dialectics gain by the injection of a third component. The third element, although possibly complicating the analysis, gives it depth. Thinkers on the conduct of war tend to pair time and space, and assess the trade-off in their interaction. Clausewitz does so too, but he also injects manpower. Moreover, space, masses and time are expressed in the theatre of war, the army and the campaign itself.[27]

Clausewitz's distinction between the military aim within the war and the political purpose of the war as a whole is a classic illustration of the dialectic process in operation: in so far as policy impinges on Books 2 to 5 (and it does not very much), the two are in tension. But both – Clausewitz points out – have to take into account a third element, the means available, which is largely set by the government (in other words, policy in action) and not by the general. In his 1804 writings, Clausewitz talked about elementary tactics and higher tactics, the first the sort of combat which small units do and the second that of larger formations. He also talked about something on a larger scale again which he called operations (although whether he meant the operational level of war as it is now understood is a subject to which we shall return in the next chapter). Policy was therefore a fourth or possibly fifth level to war. But in *On War*, Clausewitz is concerned primarily with tactics and strategy, both as single entities, and the interaction between them. When policy is included, it therefore becomes the third element. As the letters to Roeder of December 1827 make clear, policy became the means not just for developing an idea but for harmonizing it – so seeing its unity. The notion of the trinity, of three in one, so clearly stated at the end of Book 1, chapter 1, and which will be discussed in Chapter 4 of this book, therefore has a long pedigree in Clausewitz's thinking.

This polarity – between war as instrumental, controllable by human agency, and war as beyond human controls – is mirrored in Clausewitz's varied use of law as a metaphor for war. Law as practised by lawyers in litigation was not only the product of reciprocal activity between two sides, as war is, but also a set of general rules subject to modification in practice. The analogy between this sort of law and the principles of war also worked in one of the two ways in which Clausewitz used the laws of mathematics. The laws of probability played to Clausewitz's desire to systematize, to establish what is generally true or what might normally be expected to happen. But Clausewitz also used law in a more fixed, unalterable and elemental sense, as when we speak of the laws of nature. Here he was the pupil of Isaac Newton, falling back on his readings in physics and the mechanical sciences, to produce concepts central to his thinking on war, including those of the centre of gravity, of equilibrium, and of friction. These will all be discussed in subsequent chapters, but the point here is that they were intrinsic to war itself and beyond manipulation by human agency.

Even more overt in Clausewitz's methods than his reliance on law or science is his use of philosophy. He repeatedly employed the word 'philosophical' to describe his way of thinking through the problems that he was addressing.[28] But, as with his debt to military theorists, he was sparing in specific acknowledgement of those who inspired him. His 1804 notes show that he had by then already read Niccolò Machiavelli's *Discourses* (begun in 1513). Clausewitz admired Machiavelli's emphasis on the realities of power, presumably learning from him that war has a political purpose, and that war or the threat of war is ever present in the conduct of foreign policy. Clausewitz, like Machiavelli, treated war as outside moral categories, as a necessary part of governmental activity. However, the only political philosopher mentioned specifically in relation to *On War* was a figure not of the Renaissance but of the eighteenth-century French Enlightenment, Charles Louis de Secondat Montesquieu, and then only in an introductory note written around 1818. Clausewitz said that he aspired to the method of Montesquieu's *De l'esprit des lois* (1748) – 'precise, aphoristic chapters', which would attract the intelligent reader 'by what they suggested as much as by what they expressed'.[29] He achieved this in some of his early writing and again in Book 1, chapter 1. Montesquieu based his principles on the essential nature of the things he was describing. At one level, not least in its attention to the relationship between war and policy, but also in its exploration of the relationships between the different components of war, *On War* belongs in the tradition of the Enlightenment, and is indeed the culmination of its influence on military thought. Clausewitz tells us – through Marie – that it was as a result of his exposure to the work of the *philosophes* that he began the process of intellectual and spiritual awakening in the second half of the 1790s.

But by then Germany, not least in reaction to the dominance of the French language (a subject on which Clausewitz expressed himself forcefully on more than one occasion), found its own philosophical voice. Through his years in Berlin, 1801–6, 1808–11, and finally 1819–30, Clausewitz frequented exactly those circles where the ideas of the German Enlightenment, the *Aufklärung*, and its outgrowth, the *Sturm und Drang* movement, with its pointers away from rationality towards Romanticism, were current. Again, however, the connections between German philosophy and *On War* are more often expressed indirectly than directly.

The most obvious link is with Immanuel Kant. Johann Gottfried Kiesewetter, who wrote an outline of Kantian philosophy, taught mathematics and logic at the war school when Clausewitz was a pupil. It is hard to see Clausewitz as a Kantian in content: *On War* is grounded in reality and sees peace as the result of war; Kant's *Perpetual Peace* (1795) aspires to an ideal and sees peace as a moral aim. But what Clausewitz did learn from Kant was that there were two forms of truth. Formal truth united proposals with the laws of thought, and used logic to produce abstractions, which falsified reality through selection to produce an insight. Material truth united such insights with their counterparts, in the dialectical process so evident in some parts of *On War*. Clausewitz wrestled with this tension between concept and reality, seeking to reconcile them but also being aware of the distinction.[30]

Kant was over half a century older than Clausewitz. G. W. F. Hegel was only ten years his senior and died in the same year, also of cholera: the two frequented the same social circles in Berlin in the 1820s. In form and method Clausewitz may have been Kantian, but in substance he became progressively more Hegelian. Hegel's thought moved in step with the events of his times, as did Clausewitz's. In 1812, war for Hegel was an existential issue as it was for Clausewitz. But by 1827, Hegel concluded that war is fought not by individuals but by persons acting in their public capacities, as members of states. It is hard to distance this observation from Clausewitz's own contemporaneous insight on war's relationship to policy. Both men progressively incorporated other forms of conflict than those which dominated their thoughts in 1806 and 1812. Like the later Clausewitz, Hegel was interested in the relations between the abstract and the concrete, and used dialectics to explore them, even if in Hegel's case the poles in the argument excluded each other, and could only be reconciled by idealism, whereas in Clausewitz's case they tend to depend on each other. By 1827 they both realized that the conduct of war needed to reflect the fact that its object was peace and that war's purpose should be seen not as existential, but instrumental.[31]

In the fevered atmosphere of the Napoleonic wars, Hegel identified with the state, as Clausewitz did. Hegel saw it as both embodying and enabling social freedom, and argued that the individual best demonstrated his absolute freedom by putting his life at risk. Both were in contact with a third philosopher, Johann Gottlieb Fichte, who in 1814 succumbed to a fever contracted while serving with the Landsturm (a form of home guard) in the war of national liberation. Fichte's *Reden an die deutsche Nation* (1808) embodied the existential view of war in its most high-flown form: those who die in battle for freedom do not end life but give birth to freedom. Clausewitz read it when it appeared and approved of much of it, but found it too abstract and too distant from history and the world of experience.[32] None the less he responded in the following year to an article which Fichte had written on Machiavelli, and expressed himself in terms which harmonized the military reform movement with the philosophical currents to which not only Fichte but also Hegel were giving vent: 'The modern art of war, far from using men like simple machines, should vitalize individual energies as far as the nature of its weapons permits.'[33]

Clausewitz put his argument in the context of what he called 'the true spirit of war'. Montesquieu had talked of the spirit of the law, of institutions and of people; Hegel wrote of the phenomenonology of the spirit. The word 'spirit' is an important one, but – particularly in German – ambiguous. '*Geist*' can mean mind as well as inspiration; it can shade from the spiritual to the intellectual. In his 1804 notes Clausewitz used the word '*Intelligenz*' when he wished to describe the commander's rational processes, but he was at pains to say that the general did not need to be a learned person. A schoolmaster or a master-builder required far more learning; a commander needed 'very little knowledge and much exercise of judgement, very few abstract truths and many perspectives linked to the inner spirit'.[34] The early Clausewitz used *Geist* predominantly for abstractions – the spirit of the art of war, the spirit of the practice of war – but in this passage he anticipates its application in *On War*. He makes it a personal quality, a mark of character.

Clausewitz was therefore as much a Romantic as he was a child of the Enlightenment. The individual, as Hegel and Fichte also argued in relation to the state, was what gave life and meaning to the 'system' of war. Personality was not peripheral to the theory of war, but central; the same went for morale and its psychological effects. During his internment in France in 1807, Clausewitz met August Wilhelm Schlegel, who introduced him to the mystical current in Romanticism. His response to seeing Mont Blanc was the classic discovery of the Romantic: 'It is impossible to let the eyes wander with giant strides over the peaks of the rock walls, many thousands of feet high, without feeling the chest swell, the sense of potential rise and the soul fill with resolve and hope.'[35] These were the sentiments which enabled Clausewitz to tackle the tribulations of the years between Jena and Waterloo; this was the Clausewitz who told the Crown Prince in 1812 of 'the will, which in strong men dominates like an absolute ruler', and went on 'just as the light is concentrated at the centre of a fire, so the will unites the power of individuals,… bending nations before it and its awesomeness stripping the sages of their reason'.[36]

Clausewitz did not become a mystic, and the author of *On War* is more rational than the warrior of 1812. But he now largely abandoned the word '*Intelligenz*',[37] and instead used *'Geist'* almost exclusively when discussing the attributes of the commander. How *'Geist'* is read is therefore almost as crucial to the understanding of the book as is the issue of the note of 1827. Peter Paret and Michael Howard more often than not render it as 'intellect' or 'mind', rather than 'spirit'. In doing so, they reflect one aspect of the German word, but they also privilege the Enlightened Clausewitz over the Romantic. Too much can be made of the polarity, not enough of the evolution from one to the other. *'Geist'* clearly incorporates a rational element, because the audacity of the commander has to be rooted in good judgement. It is significant that what Clausewitz ultimately settles on is the idea of genius, the quality that sees through the confusion of war to its core and then takes decisive action.

Kant, in his theory of art, had dispensed with the Enlightenment's belief that genius should be set in the context of rules, and had seen it as the sole source of artistic creativity. Clausewitz, his artistic awareness given life by Marie and his sojourn in France, wrote an essay on art and the theory of art. Many of his explorations of other fields of human endeavour gave him only the metaphors which became such powerful ways of elucidating his ideas through analogy, but in this case the effect was more pervasive. Following Kant, he argued that the artistic genius does not break the rules but works within them; the truly great artist may rewrite the rules, but then the rules themselves change, and so the dialogue between genius and rules persists. Clausewitz applied these insights from the fine arts to the art of war.[38] Napoleon was a genius, who himself embodied the *Geist* of the art of war, and the challenge for Clausewitz was to find the rules which reflected the consequences of his actions. As he wrote to Fichte, 'begin not with the form but with the spirit, in the certain anticipation that this itself will break the old forms and will result in forms that are better adapted'.[39]

The title of Book 2 of *On War* is 'the theory of war'. Clausewitz aspired to write a theory of war that was not only new but also – thanks to the rigour of his analysis – usable. 'Part of the object of this book', he wrote, 'is to determine whether a conflict of living forces as it develops and is resolved in war remains subject to general laws.'[40] Like his contemporaries, he began, therefore, not with history, but with theory. His notes from 1804 are statements of theory with occasional historical references, and his serious historical output did not precede, but followed, his decision in 1816 to write a book on the theory of war. His initial inspiration came not from military history, but from his exposure to philosophy and, even more, from the fact that his own experiences of war did not match the theories that he had read. The primacy of philosophy remained fundamental to the disciplinary method which he applied to military theory and military history, and it provided the intellectual framework for an approach to theory which used reason to put the experiences of reality in order and thus to create new but verifiable propositions.

Clausewitz made clear that by theory he did not mean preparations for war or features ancillary to war. The theory of war was concerned with the use of war. Its purpose was to distinguish the different elements that make up war, and so to simplify and distil knowledge. Its essence therefore lay in study itself, exerting its influence on practical life more 'through critical analysis than through doctrine'.[41] That process, using theory as an aid to judgement, was what educated the commander. This did not mean, however, that the insights which theory vouchsafed should not be followed through to enable the establishment of principles, where that was logically viable. 'Principles, rules, regulations, and methods are... indispensable concepts to or for that part of the theory of war that leads to positive doctrines; for in these doctrines the truth can express itself only in such compressed forms.'[42] This was more likely to happen at the lower, tactical levels of war, where genius had less play, but Clausewitz did not rule it out in strategy if 'the arch of truth culminates in such a keystone... the point where all lines converge'. Principles derived from theory became vicious only when they became inflexible, when they ceased to be guides to thought and developed into prescriptive rules.[43] The commander had to know not only how to apply principles but also when to override them.

The strength of theory lay in insights rather than formulas, but its value was still rooted in its desire to generalize. In disciplines like philosophy this abstraction could be an end in itself. Clausewitz himself said that 'only a theory that will follow the simple thread of internal cohesion as we have tried to make ours do, can get back to the essence of things'.[44] But what he meant by that was the cohesion provided by the true nature of war, not by the demands of theory. The test of theory was reality, not abstract thought.[45] Clausewitz's principal reality check was his own experience, not, at least in the first instance, military history. 'Why is history so lacking in useful examples?', he querulously enquired in 1804.[46] Scharnhorst soon disabused him of this youthful cynicism, without – as his persistent side-swipes in *On War* testify – ever entirely removing it. 'The aim of historians rarely is to present the absolute truth,' he told the Crown Prince in 1812: 'they invent history instead of writing it'.[47] But he still told his young charge to read military history. War was too messy a business to permit theoretical concepts to be put fully into practice. Military history was the basis of theory and therefore its reference point. However, history, like theory itself, provided not formulas but exercises in judgement. In the final chapter of Book 2, Clausewitz concluded that historical examples could be used in four ways: to explain an idea; to demonstrate the application of an idea; to support a statement and so show that a phenomenon was possible; and to give a detailed account of a historical event in order to deduce a doctrine.

The challenge that confronted the Prussian soldiers of Scharnhorst's and Clausewitz's generation was precisely the consequence of this interaction between history and theory. The historical example of Frederick the Great had been made the basis for theory, but had then prevented the Prussian army understanding subsequent changes in the conduct of war and had led directly to the disaster at Jena. Theory, therefore, could not be based on a single example. Those 'who would construct all history of individual cases – starting always with the most striking feature, and digging only as deep as it suits them, never get down to the general facts that govern the matter'.[48]

This was what Clausewitz did not like about history, that it was built up from individual cases. He particularly disliked the phrase that there was an exception to every rule.[49] 'No matter how it is constituted,' Clausewitz wrote at the beginning of Book 2, 'the concept of fighting remains unchanged.'[50] By the end of his work on *On War*, he had become clear that whatever else he achieved it must rise above the particular and circumstantial. In Book 8, chapter 3, he surveyed the history of war, acknowledging changes in its forms over time, but concluding that something much more general – Clausewitz used the word *ganz*, meaning 'whole' and 'entire' – had to be the aim of theory.

This was not the limit of history's deficiencies. Although using history as a critic and theorist rather than as a historian, Clausewitz was sufficiently historically minded to be aware of the difficulties which sources pose for historians. Equipped with hindsight, they could see things much more clearly than could the commander on the ground, and those who were not practitioners fell back on empty phrases which sounded expert but conveyed little. Reading a general's memoirs was not likely to be much more helpful, because they tended to be selective and self-serving. Detailed and careful analyses of the sources were the corrective for these tendencies, but that requirement in turn limited the chronological range that Clausewitz could exploit.[51]

For much of the eighteenth century, military writers had cited the works of classical authors. In some instances the references to Xenophon or Caesar were just form; in others, particularly in the debate on infantry tactics as to the merits of column over line, examples from ancient history were integral to the debate. Although Clausewitz referred to Hannibal and Caesar in his 1804 notes, by the time he came to write *On War* he concluded that illustrations from the ancient world were useless. This rejection of classical precepts, in itself a breach with the intellectual methods of the Enlightenment, was prompted not only by the power and relevance of more recent examples but also by quite proper historical considerations. The problems of sources were more acute the further back in time one went. Clausewitz went on to say that only conflicts since the war of Austrian succession, which began in 1740, were sufficiently close to the conditions of the modern day. But he was certainly much less dogmatic on this point than he was on the need to recognize the weight of apparently minor elements and details, now no longer retrievable but possibly of considerable significance to the outcome. He was far better versed in the history of seventeenth-century warfare than a superficial reading of *On War* sometimes suggests. In Book 5, he took the period between the Thirty Years War and the wars of Louis XIV, and specifically the War of the Spanish Succession (1701–14), as the departure point for modern war, saying that the conclusion to the first of those conflicts, the Peace of Westphalia of 1648, marked the initiation of more recent wars. Moreover, he saw Gustavus Adophus, the king of Sweden who was killed at the battle of Lützen in 1632, as the first of 'three Alexanders' who foreshadowed Napoleon. One calculation is that Clausewitz had studied over 130 campaigns.[52]

However, there were two further constraints on the span of military history which the theorist might properly exploit. The first was practical. The emphasis on detail and the suggestion that the era of modern war could bridge a couple of centuries created the problem not of too few sources, but of too many. Theory provided a short cut, 'so one need not start afresh each time sorting out the material and ploughing through it', and this precept applied to the student as much as to the practitioner: 'we must admit that wherever it would be too laborious to determine the facts of the situation, we must have recourse to the relevant principles established by theory'.[53]

The second was the product of the dramatic change in the conduct of war wrought by the French Revolution and Napoleon. Jomini had tried to integrate the wars of the

French Revolution with those of Fredrick the Great, a process made easier by the fact that Jomini began his major study before Austerlitz was fought in 1805, and so was using early Napoleonic warfare, not the later campaigns, as his yardstick. By the time he came to the writing of Book 8, Clausewitz was clear that that was a waste of effort. This did not mean, as some critics have implied, that *On War* is focused solely on warfare after 1806, to the exclusion of the wars of the French Revolution. Clausewitz wrote his histories of the 1796 and 1799 campaigns at roughly the same time as Book 8. It is, however, a recurrent and even dominant theme of Book 8 that modern war, far from beginning in 1648 or 1740, as he had suggested in the earlier books of *On War*, actually began in 1792.

The apparent beauty of this conclusion for Clausewitz is that it seemed to open out the possibility of a reconciliation of the dialectic between theory and history. The gap between theory and practice for the Prussian army he had joined had been a consequence of the misapplication of history and had been stripped bare by the French on the battlefield in 1806. Theory was weaker, Clausewitz argued, where wars were fought for half-hearted objectives, and stronger when war was 'more obedient to the law of inner necessity'. Napoleonic war brought theory and practice into alignment. But just at the moment when this approach seemed to make synthesis possible, history reared its head once more. Clausewitz did not know the shape of future war, and therefore had no choice but to refer to the past for his models, and that made him unsure as to which form of war, the Napoleonic or the pre-Napoleonic, would recur. 'We admit, in short,' he concluded, 'that in this chapter we cannot formulate any principles, rules or methods: history does not provide a basis for them. On the contrary, at almost every turn one finds peculiar features that are often incomprehensible, and sometimes astonishingly odd.'[54]

The circular nature of Clausewitz's dialectical argument is in danger of hiding the fact that *On War* is also moving forward. That status can also be lost sight of not least when, confusingly, the opening chapter is said to be the most complete. This progression has direct consequences for Clausewitz's use of language. Clausewitz wrote in a German that favoured the passive tense, and that produced long sentences, with several dependent phrases. The scope for ambiguity that this created was compounded by his enthusiasm for words that carried several layers of meaning. *Geist* is one; *Politik*, as we shall see, is another. The challenge for any translation of *On War* is whether to be consistent, rendering the same word the same way, or whether to interpret it according to the context into which it falls. Howard and Paret opted for the latter, acquiring clarity as they did so, but occasionally at the price of accuracy and even of interpretation. Those who have preferred literalness at least have the virtue of reflecting Clausewitz's own aspirations. He appreciated the connections between theory and vocabulary, recognizing that 'in theoretical discussion, particular terms should be reserved for particular qualities'. He therefore aimed to use his work to define concepts as best he could 'to serve as an approach to greater clarity and precision of language'.[55]

A central example of how this continuous process of refinement in the use of language could operate, and could create confusion in a text that is unfinished, is the balance between ends and means, a dialectic present throughout the text and central to Books 1 and 8. In Book 1, chapter 1, this duo becomes a triad, as the ends are themselves divided into two: the military aim within the war, say the defeat of the enemy army, where the German word *Ziel*, is used, and the political objective or purpose of the war, for example, a lasting peace settlement, where the German is *Zweck*. The trinitarian aspects of this are self-evident: the military aim, *Ziel*, is the means, *Mittel*, to the political objective, *Zweck*. Moreover, it is applicable at all levels within war as well as of war: the aim (*Ziel*) of a skirmish is the means (*Mittel*) to serve the objectives of strategy (*Zweck*), and so on. Political scientists have made much of this distinction between *Ziel* and *Zweck*, pursuing it with a consistency that is not evident in the rest of *On War*. Apart from in Book 1, chapter 1, paragraph 11, Clausewitz uses the words as though they were interchangeable, and on occasion introduces entirely fresh synonyms for aim or objective, for example *Richtung* or *Absicht*. As early in the reader's progress as chapter 2 of the same book, specifically on purpose and means in war, the word that Clausewitz uses to describe the destruction of the enemy's armed forces, which following the preceding logic should be *Ziel*, or possibly – since it is a means to an end – *Mittel*, is *Zweck*. Elsewhere, even as late in the development of his argument as Books 7 and 8, *Ziel* is used of the peace itself. There are clearly moments throughout *On War* when the *Ziel/Zweck* distinction was important to Clausewitz, but this is a matter of interpretation and even subjective judgement. In Book 2, chapter 3, on whether war is an art or science, Clausewitz describes the *Zweck* of art and the *Ziel* of science – a difference which seems significant, especially in the light of the discussion in Book 1, chapter 1. But Howard and Paret in their translation gloss over the distinction entirely, and they may be justified if they are right in their assumption that Book 2, chapter 3, was written some years before the version which we have of Book 1, chapter 1, and was not revised after 1827. In Book 1, chapter 2, Howard and Paret translate *Ziel* as 'means', and then later on the same page as 'policy'. If Clausewitz had been consistent in his language, the word should be *Mittel* in the first instance and *Zweck* in the second; if Howard and Paret were being consistent with Clausewitz's own guidelines the translation should be 'aim' in both cases.[56]

The problems that the rendering of *On War* into English highlights are in some respects the problems of reading *On War* more generally. The cynic might conclude that, if Clausewitz had been vouchsafed eternal life, the book would still not be finished. That observation, at once trite but possibly true, is however more helpful than its glibness suggests. *On War*'s vitality rests in its spirit of enquiry. The fact that Clausewitz's thinking went through so many iterations is precisely what gives it strength and depth. The book is an intellectual exploration; its stimulus comes directly from the fact that it does not resolve all the issues that it raises into neat packages. Ultimately, however, the assumption which guided Michael Howard and Peter Paret in their translation was well founded: Clausewitz's mind, and especially his philosophical method, provide enough underlying unity and continuity for it to be right to treat the text as a whole, and so to acknowledge that the sum is greater even than the parts.

CHAPTER 3

The Nature of War

Two notes by Clausewitz make clear that his principal objective, at least until 1827, was not to discuss all aspects of war, but one in particular. The first, dated to 1818, states that he has addressed 'the major elements of so-called strategy', and the second, the undated note, describes the book as a manuscript on 'the theory of major war, strategy as it is called'.[1] Today the word 'strategy', used by governments to describe peacetime policies more than by armies to shape wars, has gained in breadth but has forfeited conceptual clarity. Clausewitz's definition of strategy was both narrower and more consistent: indeed it is here that *On War*'s claims to consistency principally reside. Strategy was 'the use of engagement for the object of the war'.[2] It embraced the triad of time, space and mass to decide where and when a battle would be fought and with what forces. Its focus was the conduct of a campaign within a theatre of war, not the overall purpose of the war, and it was therefore a matter for generals, not politicians. Nor was it concerned with actual combat, although that did not mean that strategy necessarily ceased to operate when the battle began. Strategy was what gave fighting significance; it exploited success on the battlefield and it created the conditions for the next battle, while victory itself was gained through combat and therefore was a matter of tactics.[3]

Clausewitz put the weight on strategy for two reasons. First, he thought it was what was most obviously new about modern war. Even a book as recent and as wide-ranging as Guibert's, published in 1772, used tactics, not strategy, in its title. In a paper written in December 1817, Clausewitz said that he found no trace of strategy in war until the reign of Louis XIV (1643–1715), and even then only in a rigid form.[4] In the end, *On War* traced strategy's roots back to Gustavus Adolphus in the Thirty Years War (1618–48). Gustavus Adolphus, like the generals of Louis XIV, had had to plan in order to be able to manoeuvre and fight. Since then, armies had become progressively bigger, with the result that the scope for strategy had expanded. In part, strategy was about scale; it was 'concerned with major bodies of troops, wide areas and substantial lengths of time'.[5] Secondly, strategy was the dominant and most important aspect of war as a whole.[6]

Tactics underpinned strategy. It is not quite true that the central books of *On War* have no dialectic. They concern the relationship between tactics and strategy, not the now much more famous dialectic of war and policy. Significantly Book 1, chapter 1, neither defines tactics and strategy nor addresses the interface between them. That itself is the clearest indication as to the importance of the 1827 note as a departure point in Clausewitz's thought. He had passed beyond the central theme of his writing up until 1827, the relationship between strategy and tactics, to take up a new one, that between strategy – or war more generally – and policy.

Ultimately Clausewitz would see war as made up of three elements, tactics, strategy and policy. In Book 2, chapter 2, he anticipated some elements of this discussion in a typical exploration of the relationship between ends and means, pointing out that the means of strategy is victory, that is tactical success, but it is strategy which gives the fight significance, while strategy is itself a means to the ultimate end of policy, which is peace. But the implications of this discussion were not made fully explicit until Book 8.[7] By contrast the relationship between tactics and strategy had preoccupied him since he was a young man. Tactics, he told Gneisenau in 1811, 'is the doctrine of the use of the armed forces in the engagement', whereas strategy, which is the essence of the art of war, 'is the use of trained armed forces for the objective of the war'.[8] The definitions in Book 2, chapter 1, of *On War* are virtually identical.

In Clausewitz's day many routine elements in the conduct of war linked strategy and tactics. Strategic manoeuvre only achieved its purposes through its tactical effects – either because it succeeded in bringing the enemy to battle or because the threat of combat induced another response. Advanced guards and outposts were on the cusp of strategy and tactics, as they detected where the enemy was, tried to divine his intentions, and then shaped the consequent engagement as the two sides converged: indeed, this shift from a strategic to a tactical function culminated in the likelihood of their being the first forces committed to combat. What in turn gave the battle meaning was the pursuit which followed the achievement of victory. Pursuit, and this was a point etched in Clausewitz's thinking by the Prussian experience in 1806, was where 'strategy... draws near to tactics in order to receive the completed assignment from it'.[9]

During the course of the twentieth century this overlapping relationship between strategy and tactics acquired a separate title of its own, that of operations. The operational level of war was placed between tactics and strategy, and became the focus for the development of doctrine in the United States after the Vietnam War; other NATO countries followed suit. Howard and Paret use the words 'operations' and 'operational' throughout their translation of *On War*, published in 1976. Clausewitz does not, and that seems to have been a conscious decision. In his 1804 notes he headed three paragraphs '*Operationsplan*', the 'planning of operations': his mention of the political objective is situated within this discussion. Yet in *On War* he eschews the word, often opting for something vague, like *Handeln*, which means 'business' or 'transaction', so stressing war's practical and everyday nature, and its place in human intercourse, or specifically *Krieg*, which means 'war'. The theatre of operations became the theatre of war, the plan of operations the plan of war. The reason for what to modern readers may appear a retrograde move in the evolution of military thought is that Clausewitz was clear that, although 'tactics and strategy are activities that permeate one another in time and space', they 'are none the less totally different'. The precise distinctions between the two might be unimportant in terms of the actual conduct of war, but they were vital to the development of theory. He saw operations, the buzz word of today's armies, as an obstacle to conceptual clarity.[10]

Book 6 of *On War*, on defence, clarified why the difference between strategy and tactics had to be maintained. In the last chapter of the preceding book, on military forces, in which he discussed the use of higher ground, Clausewitz had begun to explore the relationship between the strategic defence and the tactical offence and vice versa. Armies could fight defensively in strategic terms but offensively in tactical. The value of defensive positions, whether man-made, like fortifications or entrenchments, or geographical, like mountains or river lines, was defined by their tactical advantage. But such positions were also chosen for their strategic significance, because they commanded a major route or waterway, for example. From them the defenders might mount a purely passive tactical defence, but if they were successful they would need to exploit the results of their success by counter-attacking, an offensive action which itself could begin as tactical but might evolve into something strategic as its success grew and gave opportunities for exploitation. Ultimately what distinguished the strategic defence from the strategic offence in Clausewitz's mind was the status of the theatre of war: those defending their own territory were strategically on the defensive, however aggressive their conduct of the war within that area; those invading somebody else's territory were on the strategic offence, even if they turned over to the tactical defensive in order to hold what they had gained. This link between the theatre of war and national frontiers, first adumbrated in Book 6, was what pointed forward to the political determinants of war, and thus opened out the threefold nature of defence: tactical, strategic and political.[11]

It is in his discussion of defence that Clausewitz makes the difference between tactics and strategy explicit in the most sustained way. But it appears elsewhere. It is central to what he says about surprise, a standard principle of war in most military literature. Clausewitz regarded surprise as unimportant in strategy. A worsening diplomatic situation, preparations for the conduct of a campaign, and the geographical constraints on possible lines of advance all created warnings. Moreover, time and space were both extended in a strategic context and so undermined the opportunities for surprise which speed of movement might create. By the same token both were contracted on the battlefield and therefore tactical surprise was more easily achievable than strategic.

One way this could operate was through a second

principle central to Clausewitz's thought, that of the concentration of forces on the decisive point. However, he distinguished between the strategic and the tactical in its application. In strategy, all available forces should be massed in time and space, as 'the law of simultaneous use nearly always advances the main decision', that was to say the decisive battle. Holding back a strategic reserve, as the Prussians had done in 1806, was nonsensical, as the war could be lost in the first battle. But within the battle both time and space worked differently. A battle began with a wearing-out exchange of fire, designed to inflict casualties; the general's object should be to minimize losses in these early phases, husbanding his reserves until the point when the balance would swing, the crisis of the battle. 'The successive use of force in a tactical situation always postpones the main decision to the end of the battle.'[12] Therefore, a tactical reserve, as opposed to a strategic one, was vital. Clausewitz's examination of the allies' conduct of the Waterloo campaign both underpinned and widened these conclusions. In 1815 Wellington and Blücher had nearly delivered themselves into Napoleon's hands by dispersing too widely, allowing Napoleon to concentrate in time and space. Moreover, the Prussians had not conserved their manpower during the preceding battles at Ligny or Wavre, permitting their tactical reserves to be drawn into the firefight before either battle had reached its crisis. But at Waterloo they redeemed the situation, arriving on the battlefield late in the day, but at the crucial moment, using both surprise and reserves to maximum tactical effect.[13]

The Prussians' contribution to victory at Waterloo made a third point relevant to the distinction between strategy and tactics. 'In most cases', Clausewitz wrote, 'reinforcements are much more effective when approaching the enemy from flank and rear, just as a longer handle gives greater leverage.'[14] His image of battle itself, reflected in his accounts of three at which he had been present – Borodino, Ligny and Wavre – corroborates the notion that he is a theorist of 'old wars'. He described clashes between symmetrical forces, evenly matched and disciplined bodies of men, both bent on fighting each other, not between conventional forces and guerrillas, the latter evading combat and waging war among civilians. The prolonged fire-fight of the two opponents meant that 'the battle burnt for a long time with moderate efforts like damp powder'.[15] Fighting on parallel fronts in such circumstances wore down the other side but did not produce a decision; that depended on the tactical reserve, whose effect would be greatest if it struck the enemy in his flank or rear. 'The risk of having to fight on two fronts, and the even greater risk of finding one's retreat cut off, tend to paralyse movement and the ability to resist, and so affect the balance between victory and defeat.'[16]

At the strategic level, however, an army was less discomfited by having to fight on two fronts at once. Unlike an army in battle, it would not be arrayed in close order, but would be dispersed, articulated in divisions of (say) 10,000 men and even corps of (say) 30,000. By organizing the Grande Armée in corps, a formation of all arms, potentially as big as many armies in eighteenth-century battles, and capable of fighting an independent action for several hours, Napoleon fused strategic manoeuvre with decisive battle. In 1806 a French corps had pinned the main weight of the Prussian army at Auerstädt, permitting Napoleon to defeat the remainder at Jena, while in 1815 the French corps commander, Grouchy, had failed in a comparable mission at Wavre, ensuring Napoleon's defeat at Waterloo. For the French military theorist and historian of Napoleonic warfare, Hubert Camon, writing before the First World War, Clausewitz was a paradox: a soldier who had served in the Napoleonic wars, and who studied them deeply, yet failed to understand what Camon saw as the essence of Napoleonic warfare. Napoleon used manoeuvre, and especially his so-called *manoeuvre sur les derrières*, to ensure that he fought his battles on the best possible terms. One corps would grip the enemy from the front, while the remainder would swing to envelop him from his rear. The enemy would be forced to give battle to recover his lines of communication, but would do so on Napoleon's terms, not his own.

Clausewitz rejected the principle of strategic envelopment in favour of that of concentration. The corps system meant that part of an army could turn to face its flank and rear without the whole force forfeiting either overall unity of command or its capacity for concentration in time and space. Thus the would-be enveloper might himself be enveloped, having exposed his own flank in the bid to seek his opponent's. To do so he would have divided his forces, as part would still be needed both to pin the enemy frontally and to protect his own line of communications. Clausewitz conceded that strategic envelopment could bring about a decisive victory because it could threaten and possibly cut its opponent's line of communications. In his history of the 1799 campaign he expressed this in a typical dialectic: 'envelopment [*umfassende*] is the weaker form which leads to the greater consequences, while concentration [*umfasste*] is stronger but leads to lesser results'. Three conditions could facilitate the chances of successful envelopment: the length of the enemy's line of communications, whether that line of communications ran forward from his base at an oblique angle rather than in a straight line, and the attitude of the local population. Lengthy communications through hostile territory made an army more liable to envelopment, and these conditions themselves meant that, although envelopment implied attacking, the factors favouring its use were weighted towards the side on the strategic defensive. Here was another illustration of how the defence might find an opportunity to take up the offensive. Clausewitz believed that in strategy the risks which envelopment incurred for the attacker in the division of forces rarely warranted departure from the principle of concentration. In strategy, the central position tended to be more important than the flanks because an army's main weight would be placed there, in order to cover the most important part of the country, and the flanks would receive at least indirect protection.[17]

Moreover, Clausewitz's rejection of strategic envelopment in favour of the principle of concentration meant that he and Jomini saw eye to eye on one of the latter's best-known axioms, that of the importance of interior lines in strategy. Forces which remained concentrated could insert themselves between forces which were dispersed or divided, and could therefore bring superior numbers to bear against fractions of the enemy. Like Jomini, Clausewitz praised Napoleon's use of interior lines in his defence of France in 1814, and, again like Jomini, Clausewitz refused to endorse Napoleon's use of exterior lines – of strategic envelopment – which had brought the greatest French victories, from Marengo in 1800 to Ulm in 1805. Clausewitz attributed Napoleon's victories not to his use of strategic manoeuvre, but to his own moral force. He described Napoleon in Italy in 1796–7 as 'drunk with victory'; nothing seemed impossible to him or – increasingly – to his army; he therefore sought battle without trepidation, regardless of the balance of forces; and this lust for battle was what delivered the Austrians, doggedly believing in the effectiveness of strategic manoeuvre, into his hands.[18] Napoleon's early victories illustrated a set of principles to do with command and its nature, not to do with manoeuvre and envelopment.

Clausewitz concluded that changes in tactics resulted in changes in strategy. The original function of the corps was tactical, but its effects were strategic. The primacy of tactics went further. Only tactical success permitted strategic success, and each victory was cumulative in its significance. Tactics, in other words, shaped strategic outcomes. That was the lesson he derived from Napoleon, not that strategy shaped tactical outcomes, as Camon and pre-1914 students of Napoleon believed. In Clausewitz's eyes Napoleon's victories in battle cut through the strategic plans of his enemies, each triumph creating the conditions for the next. The allies had failed at first as they had not appreciated that, however subtle their strategy, if it did not aim to achieve decisive success in battle it was in danger of being swept away through fighting. By 1813–15, they had learned: Leipzig and Waterloo were battles which settled the outcomes of campaigns and led directly to peace.[19]

Throughout his life, therefore, Clausewitz saw combat as central to the nature of war: 'War', he wrote to Gneisenau in June 1811, 'is nothing other than fighting.'[20] Moreover, his definition of the relationship between strategy and tactics, which made strategic success conditional on tactical success, meant that tactics lead and even dominate strategy. And yet Clausewitz barely mentioned tactics in *On War*. Apart from some discussion in Book 5, chapter 4, on the relative values and uses of each of the three arms, cavalry, infantry and artillery, Clausewitz did not address the use of forces in the engagement. This was no doubt because he believed that it was at the level of tactics that routine and method were essential and that positive doctrine could be developed.[21] 'Elementary tactics', he had declared in his 1804 notes, 'are studied ten times more often – and much better – by sergeants'.[22] Sergeant he may not have been, but he was unable to avoid the subject when working for Scharnhorst between 1808 and 1812. It was presumably at this juncture of his career that Clausewitz wrote *Leitfaden zur Bearbeitung der Taktik der Gefechtslehre*. A series of 604 numbered paragraphs, this guide to tactics anticipates the succinct aphoristic style which he would eventually replicate in Book 1, chapter 1, of *On War*. In content, however, it had already moved away from the elementary tactics of the sergeant to what Clausewitz in 1804 called 'higher tactics', and whose ideas would find reflection in Book 4 of *On War*, that on the engagement.

Jomini used the phrase 'grand tactics' rather than 'higher tactics'. Here, also, more united than divided the two rivals. Jomini saw the interface between tactics and strategy in terms which were virtually identical to those of Clausewitz.[23] Clausewitz ridiculed Jomini and Bülow for their attention to the selection of bases and lines of communication, to the links between the two and what that might say for the line of advance of an army. But his definitions of both in Book 5, chapters 15 and 16, and the principles he drew from them were similar, not least for the conduct of the defence.

For Clausewitz, focusing strategy on bases and lines of

communication was wrong when it made a fetish of principles, which, while generally true – and that was their value – could not be universally so. Jomini believed that strategy could be made into a matter of routine, a positive doctrine. Clausewitz believed that was only possible in tactics. In arguing that the tactical outcome could overthrow strategy, he saw strategy as altogether more fragile than Jomini did.

Clausewitz believed that, if strategy failed to put its relationship with tactics at its core, if it did not acknowledge that its purpose was battle, and instead found its purpose within strategy itself, its tendency was to make manoeuvre not a means to battle but an end in itself. The aim became to outmanoeuvre the enemy and so make him retreat without a battle. In the twentieth century, Basil Liddell Hart, as part of his rejection of Clausewitz, praised commanders who won victories by adopting 'the indirect approach'. They, unlike the generals of the First World War, used 'the line of least expectation' to outwit their opponents rather than outfight them. For Clausewitz, this sort of thinking had condemned the conduct of war in the eighteenth century to the pursuit of half-hearted objectives. Wars between civilized countries had become 'more a matter of observing the enemy than of defeating him',[24] and so their leading characteristic – strategic manoeuvre – had been mistaken for war's ultimate purpose. Manoeuvre in ordinary usage, Clausewitz wrote, 'carries the idea of an effect created out of nothing'.[25]

Here his sarcasm was implicit. In his analysis of the Waterloo campaign it was overt. Those who wrote about Napoleon's intentions in 1815 and described his advance into Belgium as designed to separate the armies of Wellington and Blücher revealed their muddle-headedness. 'The space between two armies cannot be the object of operations' (and here he used the word *Operationsobjekt*).[26] Napoleon aimed for the gap because he expected Blücher to close it and therefore to give him the opportunity to strike the Prussian army. The enemy who was outmanoeuvred retreated because of the fear of defeat, not because of the manoeuvre itself. For the attacker, continuous manoeuvre could amount to failure. The balance of losses in a campaign dominated by manoeuvre might favour the 'defeated' army, if the latter were fighting on its own territory and falling back along its line of communications to its bases: then 'no trace of this so-called victory will show up in the final balance sheet of the campaign'.[27]

The French Revolution had broken the eighteenth-century mould not just because of the social and political changes which underpinned its wars but also because of the manner in which those wars had been conducted. Eighteenth-century armies, or at least so the conventional wisdom ran, had not been able to achieve major objectives because their supply needs had been tied to bases, granaries and depots inside their own frontiers. France had mobilized an army bigger than it could feed and supply, and had pushed it abroad precisely so that it could be fed at its neighbours' expense. Its soldiers had subsisted by looting and pillaging. But this was unsystematic and wasteful. The solution was a system of regular requisitions, organized by the army in conjunction with the local authorities. 'This method knows no limits,' Clausewitz wrote in Book 5, chapter 14, his most sustained discussion of supply, 'other than the complete exhaustion, impoverishment and devastation of the country', a development that Clausewitz, naively from the perspective of the twenty-first century, thought impossible: 'Even belligerent forces that occupy a country for any length of time will hardly be so harsh and pitiless as to place the whole burden of subsistence on the land.'[28]

Clausewitz made few predictions for the future, but he did believe that requisition would continue to dominate the supply systems of armies. In this respect the innovations of the French revolutionary armies, however uncivilized in themselves, reflected the progress of civilization. 'War, with its numerous tentacles', as he put it, 'prefers to suck nourishment from main roads, populous towns, fertile valleys traversed by broad rivers, and busy coastal areas.' Population density promoted production and the accumulation of stocks. Good roads enabled armies to move faster and more roads meant that individual corps could advance on parallel lines, dispersing to feed but uniting to fight. The more an army moved, the greater the advantage it enjoyed over the army which did not, since the latter would rapidly exhaust the produce of the surrounding area.

In his instructions to the Crown Prince, Clausewitz had suggested that logistical constraints could settle strategy. Supply determined the choice of the theatre of war and permitted the concentration of troops within it.[29] But this proposition, which harked back to the constraints of eighteenth-century war, clashed with his belief that war had been liberated from logistics. Book 2, chapter 1, while accepting that supply was significant for strategy, dismissed as secondary to the theory of war the provision of munitions and medical care. Neither is catered for by requisitioning, and both have become central to the logistical constraints under which the armies of industrialized powers have increasingly laboured. Book 5 treated the 1812 campaign in Russia, a country too backward to sustain a large army by requisitioning, as exceptional, whereas Book 6, on defence, took the same campaign as characteristic. This was a contradiction which he never reconciled. Although Book 8 embraced the Russian example, it played down the significance of supply for war plans. Clausewitz's determination to set strategy free from its logistical constraints was reflected in German planning in 1914 and in 1941, with terrible consequences not only for the populations of territories through which Germany's armies passed but also for its soldiers themselves. Clausewitz stated that the deleterious effects of privation would be overcome by good morale. 'If war is to be waged in accordance with its essential spirit – with the unbridled violence that lies at its core, the craving and need for battle and decision – then feeding the troops, though important, is a secondary matter.'[30]

The elements which Clausewitz did deem central to strategy as a whole were set out in Book 3, chapter 2, of *On War*, and were moral, physical, mathematical, geographical and statistical. All five intertwined, but the weight not only in Book 3 but throughout *On War* fell on two in particular, the moral and the physical. His experience of modern battle was that the regular armies of Europe were 'so much alike in weapons, training and equipment that there is little difference in such matters between the best and worst of them'.[31] Therefore, what settled the outcome in what today's armies would call symmetrical warfare was either superior morale or superior numbers. Of course the two could and did interact, but Clausewitz put so much stress on the first precisely because, while its importance in war had been universally recognized (not least by Machiavelli, who seems to have inspired him on this point),[32] the tendency hitherto had been to deem it unquantifiable and therefore to pass over it. Clausewitz took a common but subjective concept and put it at the centre of an objective theory of war.

Clausewitz never developed a clear conceptual vocabulary when dealing with moral factors in war, sometimes using the adjective *geistig*, referring to the spirit, and more often *moralisch*, which in German suggests moral in an ethical sense but which Howard and Paret tend to translate as 'psychological'. They share the presumption that for

Clausewitz *Moral* meant what in English is called 'morale'.[33] He used the word very broadly, encompassing factors such as the role of rumour and the impact one side's cunning had on the other. However, Clausewitz made two clear distinctions. First, courage takes two forms in war: courage in the face of personal danger, whose effects are felt in the tactical sphere, and the courage to take responsibility, a requirement of strategic success. A man who shows unflinching bravery under fire may be irresolute when faced with a major decision. The second distinction is the difference between courage, which is concerned with moral survival, and fear, which is orientated towards physical survival. Both these categorizations were carried through in the three levels at which Clausewitz analysed morale in war – those of the army, the people and the commander.

Clausewitz was comparatively uninterested in what motivated the individual soldiers of a regular army. The qualities which they enjoyed over a people in arms were those of order and discipline. Any enthusiastic outburst which usurped the steadiness of the soldier could be counter-productive, undermining the method which gave the army its order. But both were required in battle – firmness and resolution during the fire-fight, and enthusiasm in the much briefer phase of the actual onset. Discipline was not a feature either of a people in arms, which he saw as potentially stronger than a regular army, or of a commander, as his own decision to flout his king's wishes in

1812 demonstrated. Moreover, even in a regular army discipline was undermined in battle, as violence begat violence, fighting created hostility and loss of life inspired revenge. The trick was to make the experience of battle work to the benefit of morale. Although Clausewitz recognized that battle could exhaust morale, that 'soldiers, after fighting for some time, are apt to be like burned-out cinders',[34] he also believed that combat experience was a lubricant in war. He had witnessed Napoleon's army go from victory to victory, increasingly buoyed not just by its own sense of invincibility but also by each soldier's fathoming of his own personal resources. He also knew all too well how a long period of peace could atrophy an army's and a people's sense of what war required.

Clausewitz's assumptions worked for the Prussian army he had joined in 1792. The challenge that confronted both his analysis and Frederickian Prussia was how they responded to the attributes of the French nation in arms, which used patriotic passion to offset its lack of military proficiency. Clausewitz fully appreciated the power of popular enthusiasm in war (a theme which will be explored in chapter 4), and one of the strengths which he attributed to the defensive powers of a country under attack was its capacity to unite the two elements – army discipline and national enthusiasm – in one body. He concluded in terms that again reveal his attraction for the Nazis. It was necessary to counteract the 'softness and desire for ease which debase the people in times of growing prosperity and increasing trade' (as had happened to Prussia before 1813), and reckoned that 'A people and nation can hope for a strong position in the world only if national character and familiarity with war fortify each other by continual interaction.'[35]

Command was the level where Clausewitz saw moral forces playing a really important role in war, and especially in strategy. Clausewitz attributed boldness more to generals than to soldiers, but the effects were reciprocal: if generals achieved victories through their boldness they invigorated the military spirit in their armies. This was where the word *Geist* came into force, as the point was not boldness leading to rashness but boldness which 'can lend wings to intellect and insight'.[36]

Clausewitz did not see a reflective intelligence (perhaps not unlike his own) as an appropriate quality for a great commander. But the general still needed to possess the sort of 'intellectual instinct which extracts the essence from the phenomena of life, as a bee sucks honey from a flower'.[37] The German adjective for intellectual in this passage is *geistiger*, with its additional connotations of spirit and inspiration. Knowledge had to be translated into capability and decisiveness. The commander had to have 'first, an intellect that, even in the darkest hour, retains some glimmerings of the inner light which leads to truth; and second, the courage to follow this faint light wherever it may lead'.[38] On this occasion the word for intellect is *Verstand*, which could as well be translated as 'understanding', and

Clausewitz himself went on to say that he meant *coup d' œil*, a sort of inner eye which vouchsafed the ability to judge strategic as well as tactical situations. The second quality, determination, was then followed by several more – presence of mind, strength of will, imagination and statesmanship. These were all embodied in the title 'military genius', which was the subject of Book 1, chapter 3, and which encapsulated much of Clausewitz's own intellectual position. The military genius was the product of modern war between civilized powers, as primitive peoples produced only warriors. He was also a mix of real and ideal, the bridge between theory and practice in *On War*. Part of him reflected historical figures such as Frederick the Great and, especially, Napoleon, but part was a product of Kantian philosophy. Like the artist in Kant's philosophy, genius had to recognize the rules but could also make its own. 'It is a feeling, which proceeds from its proximity to and fulfilment of its own spirit [*Geist*], which in turn is strengthened by its own activity and use,' Clausewitz wrote of Bonaparte in 1796. 'When a man is seized by the effects of his own powers and convinced of the rightness of his own ideas, he develops a natural excitement for his work and a fulfilment in his execution of it. That is what fires up the poet and the painter in the creation of their works, and that is what also enthuses the great general.'[39] The romantic in Clausewitz had to embrace the military genius, the rationalist had to define him.

The moral courage of the military genius could put

defeat into perspective, using rationality in order not to be overwhelmed by the sufferings and slaughter of the battlefield in the way that the ordinary soldier might be. Clausewitz described the psychological consequences of major defeat in words that gave vent to his own searing experiences. But his message to the leader whose own moral forces were also on the verge of collapse (and hence to Hitler in 1945) was that things might not be as they seem, that the effect of defeat on the nation can be electrifying and can rouse forces that have lain dormant: 'at that point the greatest daring, possibly allied with a bold stratagem, will seem to be the greatest wisdom'.

Moral forces, therefore, could offset the effect of physical forces: morale stood in a dialectical relationship to manpower. One result of Clausewitz's call not to give up might be complete defeat. In that case, as he had argued in the 1812 manifestos, the honour that would accrue would 'at least grant one the right to rise again in days to come'. But another was the possibility of victory, even with inferior numbers. If it were invariably true that superior numbers always won, Clausewitz would have had to confront two challenges, one in the realm of theory and one in that of experience. Theoretically, he would have moved from a principle to a law of nature – from something that was generally true to something that was invariably and necessarily true. If he did that then theory would no longer be in accord with experience. Frederick the Great had sustained war successfully with inferior resources in the Seven Years

War, and he had done so precisely because he had used strategy with boldness, matching his objectives within the war to the manpower he had available. Napoleon had done so in Italy in 1796. Clausewitz's conclusion, that 'it does not follow that war is impossible for an army whose strength is markedly inferior', was inevitable not just because history told him it was so but also because as a Prussian he had no political alternative. Prussia was always likely to be weaker in numbers when flanked by France and Russia.[40]

Theory, therefore, could not permit superiority of numbers to be 'the one and only rule' or a 'permanent device', as Book 2, chapter 2, made clear. It was, however, 'the most common element in victory', according to Book 3 on strategy.[41] Here Clausewitz acknowledged, but did not yet confront, the problems of integrating his own experience with general theory. Frederick had been able to prevail with inferior numbers even when he had been unable to use strategy to achieve a local superiority on the battlefield, as the victories of Leuthen and Rossbach in 1757 testified. But the situation had changed by Napoleon's time (and therefore Clausewitz's). At the end of the day, not even the greatest military genius himself had been able to compensate for inferior numbers: Bonaparte had lost the campaigns of 1813–15 on the battlefields of Leipzig and Waterloo. Clausewitz's explanations for the consistency with which superior numbers had led to the enemy's defeat since the beginning of the nineteenth century pointed him ultimately to the exploration of the role of policy in setting objectives, a point to be found lurking in Book 5, chapter 3, and which became evident in Book 7, chapter 22. But in the interim he also found reasons for the change over time within strategy and tactics themselves. Large numbers should have exacerbated the supply problems of armies, particularly if they subsisted by requisition, and even more if they waged war in theatres that were economically backward. The invasion of 1812, if it were to be regarded as a norm, clearly had important implications for the relationship between the army's size and its supply, suggesting that in some circumstances size could be considered counter-productive. However, Clausewitz opted to see 1812 as exceptional. Napoleon was not the victim of the circumstances of campaigning in Russia, but of his own decisions. Large armies should disperse to feed, as the corps system permitted them to do, and unite to fight: Napoleon's mistake, therefore, was to advance on a single line of communications. In tactics, if battle was, as Clausewitz experienced it, a 'slow and methodical trial of strength, greater numbers are bound to make a favourable outcome more certain'.[42]

'The best strategy is always to be very strong; first in general, and then at the decisive point,' Clausewitz concluded.[43] The commander therefore had to unite his forces in time and space, but this was no more than a skill, 'the daily bread of strategy', which although vital was simply the means to an end. The crucial exercise of the commander's judgement was the selection of the decisive point.

When he came to Book 6, chapter 27, the first of four devoted to the defence of a theatre of war, Clausewitz realized that this was a choice which should be encapsulated in what he called a war plan, a subject which he then developed fully in Book 8, and that both the plan and the choice of the decisive point would depend on the identification of the enemy's centre of gravity. Each of these phrases – theatre of war, war plan and centre of gravity – now acquired increasingly specific associations.

The theatre of war was a self-contained space within which strategy was exercised over the course of a campaign. Therefore it carried connotations of time as well as space, as it took time for an attacker to traverse and in the process the defender could mobilize its immobile elements – its fortifications and its terrain – to aid strategy. Moreover, the state of its agriculture, the attitudes of its population and its prevailing weather patterns (another trinity) all had a role in shaping the war plans applicable within it.[44] By the time that Clausewitz came to Book 8, he realized that war plans could not be discussed without taking cognizance of war's political objectives, but in Book 6 he defined the war plan in terms that were more obviously strategic. It was 'the source of all the lesser plans of attack and defence, and determines their main lines; indeed, frequently a war plan is nothing more than a plan for attacking or defending the main theatre of war'.[45] Common to both treatments of war plans, in Books 6 and 8, was their role in relating means to ends. 'The first task, then, in planning for a war is to identify the enemy's centres of gravity, and if possible trace them back to a single one,' Clausewitz wrote in the last chapter of *On War*, and he went on: 'The second task is to ensure that the forces to be used against that point are concentrated for the main offensive.'[46]

Clausewitz's use of the phrase 'centre of gravity' manifested physics' function in the evolution of his theory. Again, however, it was a conception that grew in sophistication as the writing of the book proceeded, and according to the level of war which he was addressing. In Book 4, on the engagement, the major battle was 'the provisional middle point and centre of gravity [*Schwerpunkt*] of the whole system'.[47] In other words the centre of gravity was at the confluence of strategy and tactics, as strategy sought to concentrate superior forces for the achievement of victory. In Book 6, the centre of gravity 'is always found where the mass is concentrated most densely'.[48] What now preoccupied him was the relationship between the theatre of war and the armies operating within it. Consistent with his rejection of Bülow, he was not prepared to see geography itself as possessing the centre of gravity: key points in the terrain gained their significance not in themselves but from the troops which occupied them, and thus the 'real key to an enemy's country is usually his army'.[49] However, by the time he came to Book 8 he was again more conscious that what was true at one point in time might not be true at another. Now the centre of gravity developed out of the political and economic conditions of each belligerent nation. In the past the army had often been the embodiment of the state, but in Clausewitz's own day it could also be the enemy's capital or his principal ally. His studies of the campaigns in which he had himself served directly informed this new triad of army, capital and allies. The capital would matter if it were 'not merely the centre of the state powers, but also the seat of political bodies and parties'.[50] So for Clausewitz, France in 1814 and 1815 was characterized, unlike the monarchies of Europe, by party politics. Napoleon could have recovered from military defeat if he had managed to command support across the political spectrum in Paris: thus the pursuit after Waterloo and into the French capital merited an analysis as close as that of the battle itself. Conversely Napoleon's own best chance of victory lay in splitting the allies, as it was their cohesion which gave his enemies numerical superiority. In this case, as opposed to that of 1805–6, the argument about the centre of gravity lying in an alliance was proved by its cohesion.

The very last chapter of Book 8, and therefore of *On War* as we have it, is called 'the plan of war designed to lead to a total defeat of the enemy'. It is the intellectual precursor of what general staffs did between 1870 and 1945, and the rationalization above all for the hopes and aspirations of the great powers as they went to war in 1914. The first of two major principles that it laid down was a reformulation of the concept of concentration on the decisive point. It now had three parts: the identification of the centre of gravity; the concentration of forces; and the need to keep minor operations subordinate even when they represented other centres of gravity. The major operation should ideally be a single massive action, whose purpose would be the annihilation of the enemy's armed forces through battle in a victory which would result in the enemy's complete defeat. Clausewitz had adapted and refined, but not jettisoned, the basic intellectual thrust which averred that the purpose of strategy was to create the right conditions for a major battle.

Book 4, which discusses battle, is thus pivotal in *On War*, its position halfway through the book being of more than symbolic significance. The language is direct and even angry. 'We are not interested in generals who win victories without bloodshed. The fact that slaughter is a horrifying spectacle must make us take war more seriously, but not provide an excuse for gradually blunting our swords in the name of humanity. Sooner or later someone will come along with a sharp sword and cut off our arms'.[51] Such argument brooks of no equivocation. Unaffected by post-1827 revisionism or by dialectics (let alone trinities), it asserts principles which reflect directly Clausewitz's experience of late Napoleonic warfare – that the army is the nation, as it was for France and Prussia; that its defeat or success determines the fate of the state; and that a single battle can decide the outcome of the campaign, as it did at Jena or Waterloo. The link from tactics through strategy to policy was therefore direct, and sufficiently uncomplicated not to need elaboration.

Book 4 begins, in chapter 2, with a description of the battle as a wearing-out struggle between two evenly matched sides. It is then followed by a chapter which, following the means/ends relationship so central to Clausewitz, states that the 'object of fighting is the destruction or defeat of the enemy'. The German word which Clausewitz used for destruction was *Vernichtung*, literally 'annihilation' but rendered on at least one occasion by Howard and Paret as 'extermination'.[52] 'Strategy of annihilation' was a formulation which worked its way into the currency of German military thought, and which therefore for some commentators presages not just the bloody battles of the First World War but also the genocidal practices condoned and in some cases carried out by the Wehrmacht in the Second. Those who seek to mitigate the implications of Clausewitz's choice of words can find no solace in his presentation of defeat as an alternative. Further on in the chapter he defines what he means by defeat – 'simply the destruction of his forces, whether by death, injury, or any other means'.[53] The word that Clausewitz uses here for defeat, *Überwindung*, is admittedly comparatively free of the connotations of slaughter which his own definition implies, but elsewhere defeat is conjured up by more forceful words, such as *Untergang*, or 'downfall', and *Niederwerfung*, or 'prostration'.

Central to this discussion is whether the destruction of

the enemy's armed forces was the means to victory or an end in itself. In Book 4, chapter 11, which Clausewitz began with four 'unequivocal statements' about battle, he seemed to present it in terms which saw it as both: 'destruction of the enemy's forces is the overriding principle of war, and so far as positive action is concerned the principal way to achieve our object'.[54] This is Howard's and Paret's translation, and Graham's and Jolles's are very similar. But 'of war' is a gloss, and as the chapter is on the use of the battle, in a book on the engagement, it might reasonably be argued that Clausewitz intended to say that the destruction of the enemy's forces was the overriding principle not of war, but of battle, that it was a means, not an end. Here is a classic illustration of the ambiguity inherent in *On War*, and this particular one permeates the whole text, even Books 1 and 8, those in which Clausewitz acknowledged that wars might be fought for lesser objectives and in which the purpose of war was the fulfilment of policy. Book 1, chapter 2, states that 'of all the possible aims in war, the destruction of the enemy's armed forces always appears as the highest', and goes on 'the violent resolution of the crisis, the wish to annihilate the enemy's forces, is the first-born son of war'.[55] These observations clearly warrant the gloss inserted in the English translations of Book 4, chapter 11, and do little to suggest that the destructiveness of battle might be moderated by the objectives in view.

Clausewitz was aware that he could be interpreted as advocating killing for killing's sake: 'while it should not simply be considered as mutual murder... it is always true that the character of battle, like its name, is slaughter [the German word, *Schlacht*, means both], and its price is blood'.[56] However, in the same passage he reverted to the role of morale on war, saying that battle broke the enemy's spirit more than it took lives. Book 7, on the attack, devoted a brief chapter to a closer definition of what he meant by the destruction of the enemy's forces. He began with the premise that it was a means to an end, and went on to distinguish between the destruction of as much as possible and the destruction necessary to achieve the object of the attack. For Clausewitz, armies derived their tactical effectiveness from their order and therefore their destruction might mean, not physical loss, but that they had lost their cohesion beyond the point where it could be recovered. In his history of the 1799 campaign Clausewitz spoke specifically of the annihilation of the enemy's physical and psychological power.[57] Even where *Vernichtung* refers unambiguously to killing, Clausewitz could put it in terms not of unlimited but of relative loss. Mutual killing in battles of exhaustion meant that the profit of victory was to be measured in terms of numbers of deaths, and the side that had suffered fewer than those it had inflicted on its enemy would be able to count the gain as absolute.[58] Herein was the sort of logic which explained the means/ends relationship in what came to be described as attrition in the First World War. Clausewitz's problem, like that of the generals of 1914–18, was the possibility of the reverse process, the self-fulfilling and reciprocal logic which war gave to violence. He noted in Book 4, chapter 11, that in the past 'once a decision had been reached, one stopped fighting as a matter of course: further bloodshed was considered unnecessarily brutal'. But this was a 'spurious philosophy', as the recent military experience of the Napoleonic wars had shown. Victory in battle created the opportunity for pursuit. This was the victory's 'sphere of influence', which the winner had to exploit while he could. The defeated side's loss of either morale or cohesion was therefore also the means to an end – to killing more of them. Thus it would not only not be able to recover its cohesion, it would also not be able to resume the fight because of its absolute loss of manpower.

'Energy' and 'vigour' were the words that Clausewitz used to contrast the way in which warfare was waged in his own day from that of the eighteenth century and earlier. They carried connotations of speed as well as destruction. 'The nature of war', he wrote in a memorandum he sent to Gneisenau early in 1818, 'is thus a swift, unstoppable business.'[59] This idea remained central. 'Our belief then is that any kind of interruption, pause, or suspension of activity is inconsistent with the nature of offensive war,' he wrote in Book 8, chapter 4.[60] And when it came to the final chapter of the same book, the one which dealt with a war plan for the complete defeat of the enemy, the second principle – following the first, which was the identification of the centre of gravity – was the imperative to act with the utmost speed. Waiting, as Clausewitz stated repeatedly in *On War*, and particularly in Book 6, suited the defence; the offensive required speed, which was why the essence of strategy was the application of all available forces not only in space but also simultaneously in time.[61]

The implication was that wars should be short, and he saw this as another characteristic of modern war, and particularly of Napoleon's manner of waging it. 'We doubt whether Bonaparte in any of his campaigns ever took the field without the idea of crushing the enemy in the very first encounter,' Clausewitz wrote in Book 4, chapter 11. He never confronted the contrast between the short campaigns waged by Napoleon and the combined length of the Revolutionary and Napoleonic wars. Clausewitz's book may be entitled *On War*, but it no more discussed wars as entire units than did any of his historical studies, each of which focused on a particular campaign within a wider conflict. His own experience, after all, was that of short periods of fighting punctuated by longer periods of peace. Such an approach made it easier for him to be cavalier about supply, despite his recognition that requisitioning could exhaust a country; it was also why his view of war could say nothing about sea power and little about economics. In his only attempt to confront these issues, he argued that economic exhaustion would drive the belligerents to make peace, a pattern which he thought confirmed the contemporary trend to short wars, when the evidence of the Napoleonic wars could be used to suggest the exact opposite.[62] In Book 1, chapter 1, where he acknowledged that a war was not a single, sharp blow, but a succession of acts spread out in time by the mobilization of resources, by the effects of space and its consequences for concentration, and by the possible contributions of allies, Clausewitz still said that 'even if the first decision is followed by others, the more decisive it has been, the greater will be its influence upon them'.[63] This implied that Austerlitz, fought in 1805, or Jena, fought in 1806, was more important than Leipzig in 1813 or Waterloo in 1815.

Book 8, on war plans, is in fact about planning a campaign, not a war. The last chapter stresses that the first year, in other words the first campaign, carries the best chances of the enemy's total defeat. Its ideal denouement was a single major battle. Although in theory battle was a means to an end, in reality its character meant that it was an end in itself: the major battle, he had written in Book 4, was 'concentrated war'. The bigger it was, the greater its effects. Modern battles, he stressed, were fights to the finish, and their effects on morale were much greater than those of earlier wars.[64] In Book 6, chapter 28, he defined a major battle in a theatre of war as 'a collision between two centres of gravity; the more forces we can concentrate in our centre of gravity, the more certain and massive the effect will be'.[65]

Here Clausewitz leaned on a classification which he had established in Book 4. In general he eschewed the word *Kampf*, meaning 'combat' (although he used it in Book 1, chapter 2), and Book 4 itself is called 'the engagement' or *Gefecht*. Clausewitz drew a distinction between the engagement, which he used to refer to fighting which is not in itself decisive, and battle or *Schlacht*, which is. Book 4, chapter 9, discusses the *Hauptschlacht*, the major battle fought by the main forces which delivers a decision. But in Books 5 and 6 these terms, which seem to have been established on clear principles, can none the less be used interchangeably. Clausewitz refers to decisive and major engagements and to small and indecisive battles.[66] This creeping lack of conceptual clarity is a direct reflection of the clash between, on the one hand, the strong need for principles which drives Book 4 in particular, and, on the other, the need to reconcile theory with reality. Clausewitz had fought in major battles which had been decisive and settled the outcome of campaigns: Jena and Waterloo were models. But he had also been present at battles such as Borodino where that had not been the case. Clausewitz's portrayal of Napoleonic battles as protracted, attritional and indecisive, which required the successive use of force, clashed with his ideal campaign, which employed the simultaneous use of force in strategy, and reached its decision in a single climactic battle. His resolution was that war was a chain of linked engagements, and the effect of a series of engagements could equal that of a major battle, just as a battle itself was made up of its constituent engagements.[67] 'When a single impetus obtains from start to finish, yesterday's victory makes certain of today's, and one fire starts another,' Clausewitz wrote in the last chapter of *On War*.[68]

The nature of war was therefore defined in the first instance by fighting. War was a violent act to which there was no logical limit: its central feature was killing. But the killing was not purposeless: 'war', Clausewitz stated in Book 1, chapter 1, 'is an act of force to compel our enemy to do our will'.[69] The presumption both within the aphorism and in war itself was that the enemy would not accept 'our will' without a fight, for if he did there would be no war. At the heart of Clausewitz's mature appreciation of war's nature was its reciprocity. He expressed this in several ways, through metaphors which captured insights but not necessarily war's essence. He likened war to a duel, but duels involved individuals and could end without death. A battle contained many duels, all to the death. War was a form of human intercourse, 'part of man's social existence', like commerce or politics, but unlike them it was resolved by bloodshed.[70] The key point was that war dealt with reactive elements, not (as Bülow seemed to imagine) with fixed values.

The upshot was that war had its own dynamic, its own *Geist*, which existed independently of its actors. 'War must be considered as a whole,' he wrote in a memorandum which he sent to Gneisenau in March 1817 and which embraced many of Clausewitz's most characteristic insights. 'One does not speak of one commander or the other but of both together, and that is true of war as a whole;

these rules undermine time, if I dare put it that way, because the grounds on which one side holds out must be as strong as the grounds of the other for advancing.'[71] The effect of reciprocity was likely to be what is today called escalation, although Clausewitz used the metaphors of mechanics, calling them ratchet wheels, pendulums and counterweights. They operated not just as a consequence of calculation or even of the inherent nature of violence itself, although both played their part. They were driven through 'the often misunderstood' superiority of the defence over the attack, and through the lack of reliable intelligence on the enemy. The climate of war, as Clausewitz put it in *On War*, was made up of four elements: 'danger, exertion, uncertainty and chance'.[72] Three-quarters of war was wrapped in fog, and events therefore had a tendency to work against the grain of expectation. Chance was part of the climate of war.

The genius of the commander had to reckon with this. He needed luck, a commodity which Bonaparte had in abundance at the start of his career, but which had deserted him by its close: Clausewitz called the Napoleon of 1815 a gambler. The general was therefore engaged in a process which Clausewitz likened to a game of cards, another analogy which conveyed a half-truth. Real war had an element of free play which depended on interlocking calculations and decisions, each arrived at independently, but which produced their effects through their interaction. A commander might know what cards he himself held, but he could not be certain of those held by his opponent, or how his enemy might play them. He had to stake all, but he could not be sure of the ebb and flow of the game, and therefore how over time the cards might fall; gnawing at the back of his mind was the natural fear caused by 'the decisive verdict of fate'. Clausewitz spelt this out in the memorandum which he sent to Gneisenau in 1817: 'Many of these psychological issues operate in war... and the idea of playing a game [*das Spiel*] is nothing other than the commander's view of the course of war in concentrated form.' This, he insisted, was 'not an image, not a simile, but a real example,' which worked because of 'its true harmony and its close relationship'.[73] His account of the 1799 campaign, largely fought in the Alps, whose peaks he reckoned added to the aspects of 'free play' in war, was scathing in its condemnation of the Austrian commander, the Archduke Charles, for his failure to appreciate this. 'Since war is not just the pure product of necessary relations between ends and means, but always has something of the nature of a game, the conduct of war cannot avoid this element at every stage, and the commander, who has little inclination for the game, will, without anticipating it, be left behind the line and will fall into deep debt in the great account book of military success.'[74] Theory helped the commander clarify the options which the game presented. Its tendency would be to emphasize the danger of underestimating the effort required, not the reverse. The gambler's solution to uncertainty was audacity and firmness of action, offset – ironically – by a form of prudence. Given war's reciprocal nature, he would play his strong cards, and up the ante.

Clausewitz's reflections on the nature of war gain their force from the dialogue between theory and reality which his own analysis of Napoleonic war had laid bare. Battle and unbridled violence were at its core. That reflected what he had seen for himself, and he would use it as the basis for the ways in which he treated what would become pure concepts, like that of absolute war, to be discussed in the next chapter. However, the very fact that what he wrote was grounded in Napoleonic warfare was precisely what ensured his appeal to military writers and thinkers between his death and the outbreak of the First World War. *On War* emphasized the importance of moral factors, and that they could offset physical forces; this mattered to Germany, encircled in 1914 by an alliance superior in man-power and resources. It confirmed for the advocates of the offensive *à l'outrance* that a battle lost was a battle that one had believed one had lost; this resonated for armies that confronted a form of combat potentially far more awful than anything Clausewitz himself had faced. It clearly stated that the concentration of mass armies on the battlefield would bring about a decision, if not at first, at least through repetition; that too made sense in 1914. One point from *On War* that his readers perhaps forgot was that, once war broke out, its reciprocity could generate its own chain of reactions, overtaking its original purposes and generating fresh ones; to that extent they had paid more attention to Clausewitz's normative prescription, that war is a political instrument, than they realized or was sensible. Those who blamed Clausewitz for the slaughter of the First World War were not guilty of finding things in the text of *On War* that were not there.

CHAPTER 4

The Theory of War

In 1933 Basil Liddell Hart reacted to the conduct of the First World War by savaging Clausewitz for his 'doctrine of "absolute war", the fight to a finish theory', which made 'policy the slave of strategy'.[1] The idea of 'absolute war' was even more powerful in the Cold War. Its equation with an all-out nuclear exchange, a standard of 'absoluteness' unmatched by any previous conflict, gave *On War* fresh relevance. For Peter Paret, however, Liddell Hart was wrong, because Clausewitz's idea of 'absolute violence, though logically valid, was a fiction, an abstraction that served to unify all military phenomena and helped make their theoretical treatment possible'.[2] This is not quite true. In 1976, Howard's and Paret's translation of *On War* struck a chord precisely because nuclear weapons threatened to turn this abstraction into reality; in Clausewitz's day Napoleonic warfare seemed to be that reality.

Although it has been suggested that Clausewitz was introduced to the idea of absolute war by his youthful reading of Machiavelli,[3] the concept is not developed in any of his early writings. In his lectures on tactics at the war school in 1810–11 Clausewitz had used the adjective *absolut*, in the context of the defence, to mean something complete in itself, but he did not use it either of theory or of war as a whole.[4] This was also the sense in which he used the word in his discussion of mountain warfare in his history of the 1799 campaign and in Book 6, chapter 15, of *On War*. The latter speaks of 'a post small in an absolute sense, that is a post opposed by an enemy no stronger than itself'. Such a post would be capable of 'absolute resistance', which meant that it would be strong enough to deliver a decisive victory.[5] In the next chapter, which continues with the same theme, Clausewitz pointed out the value of mountains for weak forces, condemned to minor operations, and unable to seek an 'absolute decision'.[6] In these chapters, Clausewitz meant by 'absolute' something that was complete in itself but which belonged to the real world. However, by the end of Book 6 Clausewitz was confronting the crisis whose eventual outcome would be the note of July 1827. In Books 4 and 5 he had been confident that future wars would be, as the Napoleonic wars had been, 'a struggle of life or death'. Clausewitz promised to write a ninth book, which would address the fact that 'the elemental fire of war is now so fierce and is waged with such enormous energy that… regular periods of rest have disappeared, and all forces press unremittingly toward the great decision'.[7] But Book 6 had demonstrated that the logical response for a weaker power was to avoid battle. By taking to the mountains, for example, it could reduce the enemy's span of command, as the terrain would force its adversary to divide his forces not concentrate them, and so military genius would be denied its full range. Clausewitz conceded that wars in the future – indeed, not just some but most wars, a point which directly contradicted the assumptions which had guided him thus far in his intellectual quest – might be 'wars of observation'. Theory, to be of use, had to allow for this, drawing a distinction between these sorts of war and 'the kind of war that is completely governed and saturated by the urge for decision – of true war, or absolute war'.[8]

Absolute war, as first adumbrated in the concluding chapters of Book 6 was no fiction, but reality. In Book 8, Clausewitz wrote: 'we might doubt whether our notion of its absolute nature had any reality, if we had not seen real warfare make its appearance in this absolute completeness right in our own times'.[9] Chapter 2 ends by saying that theory has to give pride of place to the absolute form of war, and to treat that as the standard by which all wars should be judged. The very next chapter goes on to treat 'the absolute form of war, or one of the real forms deviating more or less from it'. The first, the absolute form, 'derives its truth from the nature of the thing', is rarely 'completely realized in any war' but can never be entirely dispensed with.[10] The second, wars which deviate from the absolute, are to be found in history, by which Clausewitz meant – as becomes clear in what follows – wars before 1792. The campaigns of 1805, 1806, 1809 and later 'have made it easier for us to form a conception of modern absolute war in all its smashing energy'.[11] In the historical survey given in chapter 3B, Clausewitz described the changes in warfare wrought by the French Revolution as a result of popular participation: 'Since Bonaparte, war, through being first on one side, then on the other, a great affair of the whole nation, has assumed quite a new nature, or rather it has approached much nearer its real nature, to its absolute perfection.' He concluded, 'The period just elapsed, in which war reached its absolute strength, contains most of what is universally valid and necessary.'[12]

Until Book 6 there had been a unitary conception of war, but Book 8, as the title of chapter 2, 'Absolute and Real War', revealed, had opened up a dialectic. Clausewitz had first asked himself whether the Napoleonic model would be applicable in future – would it be possible to 'disinvent' that which the French Revolution had ushered in? Having asked himself that question, he came to another, implicit in Book 8, if not yet fully articulated: had even the Napoleonic wars achieved absolute perfection? Both questions left him with serious problems of methodology. Clausewitz, the historian and the loyal pupil of Scharnhorst, had to acknowledge that absolute war could not be a universally applicable model for real wars, while his own experience told him that he had witnessed something akin to absolute war. He therefore wanted to find a theory which could accommodate not just one form of reality but two, the bulk of military history and his own experience. His answer was to treat absolute war differently in Book 1, chapter 1, from the way in which he treated it in Book 8; it now became an abstraction against which all wars, not just Napoleonic war, could be measured. An early draft of the chapter introduced the phrase 'a total concept of war' to express this. But the same draft makes clear that he was already toying with the vocabulary on which he finally settled.[13] The adjective, *absolut*, became, as in paragraph 6 of Book 1, chapter 1, a noun, *das Absolute*. The development is obscured because, although the idea of absolute war permeates Book 1, chapter 1, it was never accorded separate treatment; the nearest to a definition of 'absolute' that Clausewitz gave was in a paragraph on war as a gamble, where he mentioned 'absolute, so-called mathematical, factors which never find a firm basis in military calculations'.[14] In chapters 15 and 16 of Book 6, fighting could achieve absolute outcomes, but in Book 1, chapter 1, paragraph 9, wars can never reach outcomes which are absolute in themselves. Absolute war is, after all, an observation about how a war is fought, not its ends; to that extent it too lacks conceptual unity.[15]

In Book 1, chapter 1, Clausewitz the mature theorist reasserted himself over Clausewitz the historian. He returned to the form of his notes of 1804, using numbered, aphoristic paragraphs, which in this case follow a logical sequence, setting theory against reality. The driving force towards the abstraction of absolute war is reciprocity. Because each adversary forces the hand of the other, because each aspires to use all the force available to him and his opponent does the same, and because each wishes to do so through a single decision or several simultaneous decisions, war by its very nature should move to extremes, to its absolute perfection. Herein is the principle of escalation, or graduated nuclear deterrence, developed in the early 1960s by American theorists.

They found the possible use of massive nuclear retaliation incredible because of the destruction it would cause, not because it was technically impossible. Clausewitz regarded escalation as probable but not inevitable: not all wars escalate. Reasons inherent in the nature of war itself led Clausewitz to regard absolute war as an abstraction.

In his early writings Clausewitz had noted that the conduct of war was much more difficult than the principles of war – which were simple – suggested that it should be. To explain this phenomenon, he introduced the concept of friction, derived not from theory but from experience. During the course of the 1806 campaign he used it to refer to the poor command relationships within the Prussian army, but thereafter he saw lack of accurate intelligence about the enemy and his intentions, and its corollary, rumour, as the main causes of friction.[16] These formulations predated his departure for Russia, but it was that campaign which provided the evidence to back up the theory. His first draft of his history of 1812 remarked that 'action in war is like movement in a resistant element', a phrase which would find its way into *On War*.[17]

The themes of danger, physical effort and intelligence (or, more accurately, its lack), which permeate Clausewitz's discussion of *On War*, were collected together in Book 1. Friction was Clausewitz's way of squaring history with theory; it embraced the particular, and it explained why theory did not always work out in reality, but it placed both within a framework that was universal. As he made clear in a memorandum of 1817, friction brought the reality of war, that it was made up of exceptions, within a framework of rules that were intrinsic to war, not external to it.[18] An army was made up of large numbers of individuals, each with his own fears and worries, and its movements were hampered not just by its inbuilt complexities (which multiplied the bigger it was) but also by factors beyond its control, both the enemy (whose intentions the commander might or might not have divined correctly) and the weather, which itself became a metaphor for friction. It possessed only three lubricants to offset friction, all of them from the real world not from theory. One was the method and routine of positive doctrine, which could operate at the tactical level. This could be enhanced by combat experience, and, failing that, by genuinely tough training. Thirdly, the commander's genius needed not only to recognize friction in war but also to master it.

Friction prevented war achieving its absolute form, even in the hands of the 'god of war', Napoleon. But there was a further constraint on absolute war, and surprisingly this was contained in the very element which at one level was forcing war to extremes. According to the logic established by the study of Napoleonic warfare in Books 3, 4 and 5, and given Clausewitz's stress on morale and on the need to seek a decisive battle as quickly as possible, Book 7 – that dedicated to the attack – should be the denouement to *On War*, the point where theory and reality converge in the idea of absolute war. It is not; and that is the case because of reciprocity. Book 7, the least developed and sketchiest of all the books of *On War*, is in fact no more than the counterpoint to that on defence, Book 6.

Books 6 and 7 carry the dialectical form to a new level. Both in his notes of 1804 and, even more, in his war school lectures and his instructions for the Crown Prince, Clausewitz had anticipated some of the arguments relating to the defence and attack that would appear in the later work. The instructions for the Crown Prince defined a defensive war, reflecting Prussia's own position, in political terms, 'a war which we wage for our independence'. It was an option exercised by the weaker power, because the advantages of resources and geographical familiarity gave it counterweights to the perceived benefits of the offensive. But defence was only a staging post: 'we must begin, therefore, using the defensive, so as to end more successfully by the offensive'. The strategic offensive pursued the aim of the war directly, that was to say it sought to destroy the enemy armed forces, and its conduct, especially in the hands of somebody like Napoleon, was less risky than appearances suggested, as its own vigour protected its lines of communication. These ideas were incorporated in the third of the political manifestos of 1812.[19] Clausewitz was therefore clear about the strengths of the defence before he had fought in Russia, but the bias of his argument was still tilted in favour of the offensive as the final purpose of war. This was reflected in the key dialectic of Books 6 and 7, that the defensive was the stronger form of war with a negative aim, while the offensive was the weaker form of war with the positive aim.

Although Bülow had anticipated some of this in pointing out the strength of a nation engaged in self-defence, Clausewitz felt that what he was saying was genuinely novel, and his propositions have proved problematic for military theorists ever since. The attacker of Book 7 is on the strategic offensive; in other words he is invading enemy territory. Clausewitz describes his advance; he is more exhausted by each battle than is the defender; his lines of communication lengthen and his flanks become exposed; his manpower is diminished not only by battle but also by the need to protect his rear and to suppress the defence's fortifications and strong points. The local population turns against him, at best denying him supplies and at worst harrying him and so forcing him to disperse his forces. Rather than acknowledge the value to the attacker of feeding at the enemy's expense, Clausewitz turned the case for requisition on its head. The attacker's utilization of his own victory eats up the very advantages which it has given him. In his account of the 1814 campaign he admitted that a fresh victory would give a new sphere for strategic exploitation, but he did not allow for this in *On War*, and he did not concede the usual argument in favour of the offence, that the side which takes the initiative can select the decisive point and concentrate its forces accordingly.[20] He did acknowledge that the attacker would gain in morale from the elation of success, but even that advantage was seen as transitory, and would be overwhelmed by the swing of the pendulum in favour of the defence. Most remarkably, given his own experience of alliances in the Napoleonic wars and his lack of faith in their robustness, he argued that allies would rally to the side that is defending and ostensibly weaker, and not to the winning cause. Ultimately, and this stage is reached in Book 7, chapter 22, the attack reaches the culminating point of victory. His study of the Italian campaign of 1796–7 used this idea to explain why the French had not pressed on into Vienna; they had tailored their ambitions to their means. Book 7 concludes by arguing that all campaign plans will therefore aim for the point where the attack turns into defence. In Book 8's last chapter the military genius is still expected to conform to the expectations of absolute war by pushing forward to the achievement of decisive success in the shortest possible time, but in Book 7's last chapter he is being told not to overshoot the mark and to judge the point of equilibrium where the balance of advantage will swing to the defence.

Book 7 does not so much lead into Book 8 as follow out

of Book 6. The positive aim for the defender is to hold what he has gained through the attack, but the attack which goes over to the defence – in conformity with the idea of the culminating point of victory – adopts the defensive in its weakest form and is therefore particularly vulnerable to counter-attack. Clausewitz made value judgements which stacked the cards against the attack, but he did so for reasons which did more than reflect his own political need to explain how and why Prussia could resist Napoleon. War, he pointed out, begins with defence. The offensive does not lead to war unless the side which is attacked responds; this is why reciprocity is central to understanding war's nature. The big advantage enjoyed by the defender is time.

The youthful Clausewitz, marvelling at France's conduct of war, had seen its ability to concentrate forces in time as even more significant than Frederick the Great's ability to concentrate forces in space. Attackers, he concluded, could not gain time, they could only lose it, as the Austrian commander Leopold Joseph von Daun had done by postponing battle in the Seven Years War.[21] Napoleon's campaigns were short, relying on speed to carry out the attack. In *On War* speed is a consistent characteristic of the offensive, especially in Book 8, on war plans. But Book 3, on strategy, has a chapter on the suspension of action in war. Clausewitz, still at this stage of his writing dominated by the Napoleonic model, described a pause in active hostilities as a contradiction in terms, a point which he would specifically rebut in Book 1, chapter 1, paragraph 14. He could think of three reasons (yet another trinity) to explain these pauses: fear leading to indecision, imperfect intelligence, and the greater strength of the defensive. As this third point grew in importance with the writing of Book 6, so did his awareness of wars where activity was suspended. Book 6, chapter 28, acknowledged that 'a great majority of wars and campaigns are more a state of observation than a struggle of life and death'.[22] The decision was postponed more often than it was sought; most wars were made up of a succession of blows, not a single strike. The reason was that waiting worked to the advantage of the defence, a principle that was the necessary corollary of that of speed for the attack. Here theory prevailed over the circumstantial evidence of individual campaigns. In 1814, as Clausewitz had acknowledged in his own account, time did not work to Napoleon's advantage in the defence of France, but did give the coalition greater opportunity to assemble their forces for the offensive.[23] Principles were what was generally true, not universally so.

The qualitative distinction of defence lay not in what it conveyed about fighting, which looked much the same whether one was defending or attacking, but in waiting. Time, Clausewitz argued in Book 6, was the characteristic common to the two chief methods of resistance. Either the defender fought the attacker early in the campaign in a battle close to the frontier, or he delayed battle and retreated into the interior. In the first case, where time was short, casualties were inflicted on the attacker by fighting; in the second case they were inflicted by the strains of a prolonged advance. The defender gained, Clausewitz said in a reference to the parable of the talents in St Matthew's Gospel, where he had not sown. Fortifications, whose science had been ridiculed by Napoleon's disciples as an over-worked hobby-horse bypassed by the speed of modern war, were seen by Clausewitz as gaining time for the defence.

The offence was complete in itself, in that the attacker used it at all the levels of war, strategic and tactical, and in doing so it achieved the purposes of the war. Defence, on the other hand, was only relative. Clausewitz rejected pure and passive defence as contrary to the waging of war, which involved the reciprocal exchange of blows. He therefore embraced the strategic defence but not the tactical. 'If one wanted to limit the concept of the defensive to complete passivity, it would result in complete absurdity,' he had told his pupils at the war school in 1810. 'If there were two fighters, of whom one always thrust and the other always only parried, there would be a sort of war in which only one side conducted war.'[24] Because war was in fact reciprocal – he had concluded by the time he wrote Books 6 and 7 of *On War* – eventually the attacker would reach the culminating point of victory and the defender would be able to go over to the attack himself. The use of the tactical offensive would create the opportunity to abandon the strategic defensive for the strategic offensive. This is what had happened in 1812; it was what Clausewitz would like to have happened in 1806; it was what Napoleon ought to have done in 1814 if he had been able to tailor his ambition to his means.[25] But in elevating 1812 from history to theory Clausewitz ran into the limitations of his own method. His presumption that the damage done to the interior of the country would be acceptable and that the population would take up arms against the invader, like the argument that allies would come to the aid of the defence not the offence, worked for Russia, but did not apply to Prussia in 1806 or to France in 1814. His answer to this charge was that the mobilization of the people for a war of national resistance could not be improvised, but required careful and lengthy planning.

Book 6 brought Clausewitz face to face with the role of policy in war. Its opening chapter began with a threefold division of war which contrasts with the earlier emphasis on the bilateral relationship between strategy and tactics. Now 'the whole war' and 'the whole country' were placed over the campaign and the theatre of war, which lay in the domain of strategy. Moreover, defence itself was defined not just in tactical and strategic terms, but also in political. The ultimate objective of the attacker was the possession of territory, and the purpose of the defender was to thwart the attacker's intentions by protecting his territory and securing a favourable peace settlement. Ensuring the security of one's own citizens or achieving victory on the battlefield was no more than a means, not an end in itself. The implications of this argument led Raymond Aron to conclude that, if Clausewitz had lived long enough to return to Book 6, it would have become the basis of a theory of conflict resolution. However, this was not how Clausewitz saw it from the perspective of Prussia's position in 1812: opening the war with a pre-emptive strike, by launching a preventive war, best fulfilled the political objectives of defence.[26] Aron's attention to Book 6 does, however, point to a more sustainable conclusion in relation to the text as we have it. War in Book 6 is much less decisive than war in the immediately preceding books. If defence is stronger than attack, and if the defender who successfully goes over to the counter-attack himself eventually confronts the culminating point of victory, war, at least in theory, cannot deliver major outcomes. The result is that Book 8, on war plans, has three chapters devoted to war with restricted objectives. Moreover, Book 8, chapter 3A, which discusses not wars that are limited but wars that aim to be decisive, says that the more wars approach the absolute the more they must be planned right through to their final outcome. Here theory, even wishful thinking, seems to be asserting itself over reality. Apart from its presumption that a decisive war must be sufficiently short to prevent the war developing its own dynamic, chapter 3A also ignores the effects of reciprocal action and of friction, both of them calculated to upset such a rigid approach to war planning.

The recognition that war might not of itself be able to deliver its most grandiose objectives forced Clausewitz to reconsider the relationship between war and policy. Not until Book 8, and then Book 1, whose final form is assumed to postdate Book 8, did Clausewitz give this topic the sustained attention which the subsequent reputation of *On War* would lead the reader to expect. The relationship between strategy and policy is an insignificant element in Books 2, 3, 4 and 5, especially by comparison with the recurrent references to the relationship between strategy and tactics. True, Clausewitz acknowledged at the beginning of Book 3 that at its highest level 'there is little or no difference between strategy, policy and statesmanship'.[27] The context seems to be that of international relations, of war's use in the furtherance of foreign policy, not that of domestic politics. Of the latter, Clausewitz says little before Book 6 beyond his observation that the government's task is to settle the size of the army, which the general must accept as a given. His job is to do the best with what is put at his disposal, through the exercise of strategy.[28] Book 4, chapter 3, on the engagement, begins with the assertion that the political object is the ultimate aim of contemporary warfare, and the point is repeated in the same book's chapter 8, but it is not followed through and efforts to find it elsewhere in these books depend on glossing the text.[29] There is scant recognition of the theory either that war is subordinate to policy or the notion that the general is subordinate to the politician in how he conducts it. Even in Book 6 itself, in chapter 28, on the defence of a theatre of war, Clausewitz says that the general will first select an objective, and then 'judge how circumstances of geography, statistics and politics, and conditions of materiel and personnel in his own and the enemy's army will fit into it, and he may then adjust his plans accordingly'.[30]

Unlike strategy and tactics, both of which are regularly and consistently defined, Clausewitz avoided close definitions of policy and politics – and this is not just a reflection of the fact that ambiguity is inevitable when the German word *Politik* means both. 'Policy unites and reconciles within itself all the interests of internal administration and also those of humanity and of whatever else the philosophical mind might bring up,' Clausewitz wrote in Book 8; 'for it is nothing in itself but a mere representative of all these interests towards other states.'[31] Here, as elsewhere, if *Politik* is translated as 'policy', it implies national and even foreign policy. In most contexts that is right. For Clausewitz the purpose of national policy was to be strong in foreign policy. A creed committed to paper in 1805 makes this clear: 'For me the chief rules of politics [or policy] are: never be helpless; expect nothing from the generosity of another; do not give up an objective before it becomes impossible; hold sacred the honour of the state.'[32]

Here he reveals his debt to Machiavelli, and it was also to early modern Italy that he traced the origins of the idea of the balance of power, which, although by his own day extended to all Europe, 'only reveals itself when the balance is in danger of being lost'.[33] That was clearly the case with Napoleon's domination of the continent. Clausewitz read the work of the balance of power's principal theorist, Friedrich Gentz, soon after 1806. In *On War*, he provided a full description of how he saw the international system operating: 'We do not find a systematically regulated balance of power and of spheres of influence, which does not exist and whose existence has often been justifiably denied; but we certainly do find major and minor interests of states of peoples interwoven in the most varied and changeable manner.' This balance of power, which emerged spontaneously, was therefore not unlike such specifically Clausewitzian concepts as the centre of gravity and the culminating point of victory; it was a physical and mechanical response, which operated like a law of nature, independently of human endeavour. Its effects were 'to maintain the stability of the whole rather than to promote change' and 'to keep the existing order intact'.[34] Significantly the discussion of the balance of power occurs in Book 6, on the defence, thus revealing why war and politics interact. A defending state would have allies because the invasion of its territory would call the balance of power into operation, and as a result advantages would accrue to the defender which explained not only the inherent strength of the defence but also why great attacking commanders, up to and including Frederick the Great, had to be content 'with moderate success'.[35]

If *Politik* is translated as 'politics', the modern reader is inclined to read that as a reference to domestic and even party politics. Clausewitz never seems to be referring to party politics in *On War*.[36] In his accounts of the 1814 and 1815 campaigns, party politics were important to his portrayal of Napoleonic France and he identified them as such. Moreover, as he acknowledged in Book 8, in the 1790s French party politics, driven by social revolution, transformed war itself. Such powerful domestic pressures could clash, rather than converge, with policy. Friction could therefore be a problem inherent within *Politik* as well as within war. These were points whose implications Clausewitz opted to duck, not least in Book 8 itself, on the formulation of war plans. Here he treats policy as unitary, free of friction, and clearly focused. He specifically states that policy aims to overcome party interests, and goes on, 'here we can only treat policy as representative of all interests of the community'.[37]

The government's role, not least in a monarchy, was to unite those interests. Sometimes in *On War* he used the word *Volk*, meaning both 'nation' and 'people', to convey just such a union. In the context of governmental policy, however, he used either *Staat*, meaning 'state', or, much more often, *Kabinett*. 'The soul of war', he wrote when putting the case for the Landwehr in 1819, 'resides in the cabinet.'[38] But, as with modern readings of the word 'politics', it would be mistaken to see this as indicating Cabinet government as we understand it today. In his account of the 1806 debacle, Clausewitz attributed a large measure of responsibility for Prussia's defeat to Cabinet government. Under Frederick the Great, Cabinet government had worked because he was a strong king who ruled by decree. His Cabinet was made up of his personal advisers and close staff. Indeed, the very idea of war's use as an instrument of policy becomes even more of a truism when set in the context of Frederick's reign, since he combined both political and military power in one person. He might consult his ministers, but he did not forfeit his powers of decision; the Cabinet was not an executive body. After his death, Prussia was left without clear direction. Ministers were asked questions and gave answers, developing their own points of view, but were not guided to a common goal nor did they take full responsibility for their actions. 'The worst aspect of Cabinet government is that it enables the prince to do nothing, as though he had a prime minister, without the advantages of one.'[39]

The weakness of Cabinet government in relation to strategy was therefore a pressing concern for Clausewitz. His later historical works criticized the role of the French Directory in the 1796 campaign and of the Austrian Cabinet in 1799. The latter never appreciated the consequences its decisions had in the theatre of war, failing to realize the reciprocal effects which ends and means have in war's conduct, and that the means – that is fighting – could never be considered as a lifeless tool. For those in the field, the original political purpose was far less pressing than the immediate motivations of battle. His conclusion must surprise those who see Clausewitz's later analysis of war and policy solely in normative terms: 'most well conducted wars will be led on the basis of the subjective convictions of the commanders'.[40]

This helps put Book 6, chapter 26, of *On War* in context. 'A government [*Staat*]', he wrote, 'must never assume that its country's fate, its whole existence, hangs on the outcome of a single battle, no matter how decisive.'[41] In 1806 the Prussian government had failed to distance itself from the drama of the battlefield. In Book 3, chapter 1, Clausewitz said that strategy used to be settled in Cabinet but that this was only acceptable if the Cabinet was in the field, close to the army, and could therefore function as a general headquarters. Although he never wrote the chapter on the structure of supreme command which he promised in Book 8,[42] he did give some indication as to his thoughts in that book's chapter 6, on war as an instrument of policy. He said that the major lines of modern war were set by Cabinets, that is to say political, not military, bodies. Therefore the Commander-in-Chief should be in the Cabinet, so that the Cabinet could share in the making of strategy. For this to be effective the Cabinet should be close to the theatre of war. The text of this section was altered between the first and second editions of *On War*, in order to suggest that the Commander-in Chief should take part in all the Cabinet's important decisions, including by implication decisions that were outside the war itself.

Much more has been made of this textual alteration than the overall context provided by the rest of *On War* warrants.

The original is now seen as endorsing liberal democracy's subordination of the military to political control, which is indeed the conclusion to be drawn from what Clausewitz said about war being a political instrument. But Clausewitz emphatically did not see the general as a political neuter. The Commander-in-Chief, he declared in Book 2, chapter 2, 'must be familiar with the higher affairs of state', and in Book 1, chapter 3, the military genius 'requires a keen insight into state policy in its higher relations'. Clausewitz was discussing a general's role not in domestic, but in international policy: 'The conduct of the war and the policy of the state here coincide and the general becomes at the same time the statesman.' Strategy opened out so many more possibilities than tactics precisely because it led directly to peace.[43] Clausewitz's focus in Book 8, chapter 6, is therefore less the issue of military subordination than of civil-military harmonization. Those responsible for policy need to have sufficient grasp of war's true nature not to make demands of war which war cannot fulfil. Generals who bridled at political intervention in matters of strategy failed to see the actual nature of the problem, which was not that such interference was harmful or illegitimate – it emphatically was not. What offended them was that the proposed policy was not in harmony with strategy, with war's nature, and was therefore built on false foundations. 'If the policy is right – that is successful – any intentional effect it has on the conduct of the war can only be to the good. If it has the opposite effect the policy itself is wrong.'[44]

Book 8 exposed a further realization – that the French Revolution had made war a matter not just of Cabinets but of the entire nation, the *Volk*; 'suddenly war again became the business of the people – a people of thirty millions, all of whom considered themselves to be citizens'.[45] At first France's opponents were slow to appreciate the political underpinnings that had transformed France's methods of fighting, preferring to look for explanations that were tactical or narrowly military, but the impact of Napoleon's conquests caused war's reciprocal nature to assert itself. 'The means then called forth had no visible limit, the limit lost itself in the energy and enthusiasm of the governments and their subjects.'[46] Therefore the effect of policy on war, as described in Book 8's recent history of war's conduct, is not to limit war, as later liberal interpreters might wish the text to read, but to remove restraints. The Napoleonic wars revealed the nature of absolute war because policy was in harmony with war's true nature. The conclusion here is not that war should adapt itself to policy but that policy must adapt itself to war. Clausewitz ended Book 8, chapter 3, by saying that 'the aims a belligerent adopts, and the resources he employs', will be governed by three factors (another triad): 'the characteristics of his own position', 'the spirit of the age', and 'always... the general conclusions to be drawn from the nature of war itself'.[47]

The corollary of this conclusion was that the tensions between war and policy were less evident in major wars. Once again Clausewitz the theorist had to confront

Clausewitz the historian. How was he to account for wars whose aims were not in harmony with war's true nature, where the objectives were half-hearted and could be fulfilled without the destruction of the enemy on the battlefield? In his portrayal of eighteenth-century war, strategic manoeuvre and its avoidance of major battle were the consequence of the political motivations driving the war, not of strategy per se. Policy therefore explained why wars before Napoleon had not conformed to the expectations of absolute war. But what this meant – at least when he was writing Book 6 – was that policy stood outside war. Rather than being integral to its nature, it operated in opposition to it. In his history of the 1814 campaign, the diplomatic considerations which dogged the allies, although not as prevalent as in wars before 1789, were 'like alien elements weaken[ing] the speedy fire'.[48] The general who adopted the defensive in Book 6, and therefore embraced limited objectives, did so only because his weakness left him with no other choice. Once the forces had been equalized he would adopt objectives that were consonant with war's nature and pursue the destruction of the enemy. As Clausewitz put it, even as late in his writing as Book 8, chapter 6B, 'war is simply a continuation of political intercourse, with the admixture of *other* [my emphasis] means'.[49] Policy, as it is portrayed in Book 8, does not necessarily penetrate war at every level. It shapes the war plan, but not tactics. It may provide the logic of war, but war still has its own grammar (to put a familiar phrase from this chapter in a somewhat different light). Policy, therefore, tends to stand outside war, making it a 'half-thing', as opposed to a 'whole' war.[50] This was exactly the phrase that he used of a real event, the naval battle of Navarino, fought by the British against the Turks in support of Greece's independence, on 20 October 1827, just as he was formulating these ideas.[51]

However, Book 8, chapter 6B, stands on a cusp in Clausewitz's thinking about war's relationship to politics. He could not leave himself with the philosophical incoherence of wars that had taken place in the past and that might recur in the future that were not conceptually entire. His answer was that policy itself provided the unity that wars in their diversity could not. In one of the last of his historical studies, that on the Waterloo campaign, he interpreted policy as more central, and developed his treatment of it. 'The forces and effects, means and aims, brought forth in strategy always drive deeply into policy, the greater and more embracing they become, but as a modification of political intercourse, as a carrying through of political plans and interests through the realm of combat.'[52] Here he was interpreting history in the light of what theory had led him to conclude in chapter 6B: 'If war is part of policy, policy will determine its character. As policy becomes more ambitious and vigorous, so will war, and this may reach the point where it attains its absolute form.'[53] This formulation reflected what had occurred in his own experience. But policy could equally well pull war in the other direction. A passage in chapter 6A, whose ambiguity presents problems for the translator, seems to encapsulate this duality, positing two forms of war, a war without political limits and a war with them, united by the common denominator of policy. Clausewitz wrote: 'Once one allows for the influence of policy on war, as one must, so there are no more boundaries, and one must allow oneself to bring war to such levels where it consists in a mere threatening of the enemy and an undercurrent of negotiation.'[54]

In 1804 the young Clausewitz had allowed for policy setting war two sorts of objective. One was a war which aimed to destroy the enemy army and its state, the other one in which the victor could dictate (not negotiate) the terms of peace. The overall purpose of the war, the final peace settlement, and the objects of strategy, the means to that peace, were therefore confused, especially when the 'nearer aim of the war' was also the destruction of the enemy's armed forces.[55] However, all that happened between 1804 and 1815 confirmed the reasonableness of this conflation. According to Clausewitz's instructions to the Crown Prince there were three main objects in war (an early trinity): the destruction of the enemy armed forces, the seizure of his material sources of strength, and the influencing of public opinion; but the achievement of the first would tend to settle the other two.[56]

The older Clausewitz, free from the passions of war's immediacy as he laboured on the final chapters of *On War* in the tranquillity of his study, played with the same stock of ideas but with very different priorities. Book 8, chapter 1, on war plans, began with the same premise as that established in 1804 and 1812: 'the overthrow of the enemy, consequently the destruction of his military forces, is the chief object of the whole act of war'.[57] However, he now developed an idea which he had hinted at in 1804, but not then followed through, and probably – given the events of 1806 – had even temporarily lost sight of. The best way of destroying the enemy armed forces, he had gone on to say in 1804, was to secure part of the enemy's territory so as to secure his resources for waging the war. Frederick the Great had waged war on this principle, and it is therefore unsurprising that the writing of Book 6, in which the Prussian king figures so prominently, caused Clausewitz to return to the theme of territorial control. The ultimate object of attack and defence, according to Book 6, chapter 7, is possession. At the end of Book 6, chapter 27 considered the armed forces simply in relation to territory: the former protected the latter, and the latter sustained the former. If, as a consequence, the object of the war became the possession of territory, rather than the destruction of the enemy armed forces, battle was no longer essential, and war might become less decisive. This thought was carried through into Book 7. Having described a campaign in Book 6 in terms of territory defended or forfeited, Clausewitz defined the attack in terms of its conquest – from that of a small province to that of a whole country. The principle of the value of territory as an object of war had implications for war's conduct. If both sides were set on mutual defence of their frontiers, waiting would prevail on both sides, battles would be avoided and destruction would be limited. This would be especially likely if the attacker recognized the effects of the culminating point of victory. Such fighting as did occur would not lead directly to peace, which would instead be the product of negotiation during the period of waiting.

The effect of elevating the importance of territory as an object in war was to minimize the role of political purposes in motivating war. Wars for the survival of the nation, which were reflected not just in the writings of 1804 but also in the political manifestos of 1812, dropped below Clausewitz's horizon. Book 8 interpreted political ideologies as having changed the way in which the war was conducted, but not the reasons why wars were fought. For Clausewitz, the ultimate purpose of war was peace, which like war could not be a 'half-thing'.[58] However, whereas the purpose in 1804 was to dictate the peace to a prostrate enemy, by the time Clausewitz came to write about the culminating point of victory in Book 7, chapter 22, the aim was to create a military situation sufficiently favourable to give a relative advantage in the negotiation of peace. The destruction of the enemy's armed forces or the seizure of his territory were not the aims of the war but the means to opening the door to its cessation.

As a result, the effects of policy as adumbrated in Book 1, chapter 1, of *On War* are altogether more benign than those allowed for in Book 8. In the ninth section of the chapter Clausewitz seems to come to the somewhat pessimistic conclusion that the result of war is never final, thus allowing for the renewal of hostilities. In fact his point is at once both philosophical and more optimistic. He argued that the verdict of war was never in itself 'absolute', since the defeated state would regard it as transitory, but he suggested that therefore a long-term solution had to be found in the policies pursued subsequent to the peace. In the very next section, entitled 'the probabilities of real life take the place of the extreme and absolute demanded by theory', Clausewitz went on to say that 'in this way the whole field of war ceases to be subject to the strict law of forces pushed to the extreme'. Once the law of extremes in war, 'the intention of disarming the enemy and overthrowing him', lost sway, 'the political object of the war once more comes to the front'.[59] Clausewitz still allowed for wars of national existence in which policy would be less evident because it would be acting in harmony with war's true nature, which itself would more closely approach the ideal of absolute war. But the latter had now become an abstraction, and wars of national survival the exception, not the rule. If war were 'a complete, untrammelled, absolute manifestation of violence (as the pure concept would require), war would of its own independent will usurp the place of policy the moment policy had brought it into being; it would then drive policy out of office and rule by the laws of its own nature, very much like a mine that can explode only in the manner or direction predetermined by the setting'.[60] But Clausewitz did not now see war like that. War sprang from a political purpose and policy would remain the supreme consideration in its conduct: 'policy, therefore, will permeate the whole action of war and exercise continual influence upon it, as far as the nature of the explosive forces within it allow'.[61] In Book 1, Clausewitz argued that in real war policy permeates the entirety of its action, acting as a moderating influence, and – along with friction – preventing it from reaching its absolute ideal. But he had elided what he now felt policy should do to war with what policy actually does to war. In practice policy adapts to war, to its development and circumstances, as much as war adapts itself to policy. The dynamics of war, which Clausewitz had explained so graphically in earlier writings, could make the policy which had given rise to war inoperative, forcing the policy, not the war, to change direction. This was the function of strategy, which is precisely what the bulk of *On War* is about. In Book 1, chapter 1, Clausewitz the theorist had prevailed over Clausewitz's own experience, with the result that he presented norms as realities.

Book 1, chapter 1, embodied a rational and instrumental approach to war. But it also contained within it the seeds of an argument which both rescued Clausewitz from the tyranny of his own normative prescriptions and has helped explain Clausewitz's continuing importance for strategic thought since the end of the Cold War. In its eleventh section, entitled 'the political object now comes to the fore again', Clausewitz explained how the political purpose determined both the military objective and the scale of effort required to achieve that objective. The greater the predominance of the political purpose, the more – if that purpose was reduced – would the war also be reduced and the more evident would be its political purpose. But policy was not necessarily determinative: it was subject both to politics and, even more powerfully, to the nature of war itself. Amid all his rationalization, Clausewitz still acknowledged that war by its very nature possessed its own escalatory dynamic, what he had called 'the explosive forces within it'. These were more likely to be put into operation when the populations as a whole were involved: 'Between two peoples and states such tensions, such a mass of hostile feeling, may exist that a motive for war, very trifling in itself, still can produce a wholly disproportionate effect – a positive explosion.'[62]

Clausewitz introduced here a polarity between policy and passion, between government and people, which was developed and resolved in his best-known trinity. The very last section of Book 1, chapter 1, a mere half page on the consequences of what had gone before for theory, described war as a something that continually changes its characteristics. It consists of three dominating tendencies, which work in different and variable combinations in each concrete case – 'violence, hatred and enmity, which are to be regarded as blind natural force' and are the essence of war; 'the play of probability and chance within which the creative spirit is free to roam'; and 'its element of subordination, as an instrument of policy, which makes it subject to reason alone'.[63] No one of the three elements is continually dominant, not even policy. Clausewitz used a metaphor from physics to explore this relationship, likening each of the three to a magnet, with the theory of war suspended between them, as they both attracted and repelled each other. However, unlike many of the other triads which litter *On War* and are not necessarily intimately linked, this trinity, like the Christian trinity, really is three elements united in one. Clausewitz used the adjective *wunderlich* to describe it. Howard and Paret translate this as 'remarkable', but this understates the force of the epithet, which given its mystical connotations could be rendered more appropriately as 'wondrous' or even 'miraculous'.

Clausewitz then went on to associate each of these attributes with three components of the state at war. It was these, rather than the attributes themselves, that so appealed to Colin Powell and other Americans after the Vietnam War. The second, that linked to the issue of moral qualities, *Geist* and courage, was the province of the army and the military genius at its head. The third was the government, which by remaining detached from the battlefield directed policy along rational lines. The first, however, was an attribute of the *Volk*, the entire nation, since the passions which war kindles must already be present in the people.

The shift from the original trinity of moral attributes to a trinity of specific actors makes plain why the commentators on Clausewitz of the late twentieth century tended to privilege the political and rational over the passionate and popular. The second and subsidiary set are the tools of a nation that opts to wage war to achieve a specific set of objectives, not features of war itself. War involves reciprocity: even at its most rational it can never itself be an act of policy as it is the intention of the enemy to confound efforts to implement that policy. Put crudely, in war two trinities clash with each other, and it is the conflict between the three elements of each which generates the scope for friction and escalation. Where policy is pitted against passion, where hostility ousts rationality, the characteristics of war itself can subordinate and usurp those of the 'trinity'.

Until 1976 few Clausewitz scholars devoted much attention to this brief and underdeveloped section on the 'trinity'. Raymond Aron made it central to his study of Clausewitz, *Penser la guerre, Clausewitz*, but he concentrated on the rational element and neglected both the people themselves and their potential for irrationality. However, particularly since 1990 and the Cold War's end, the trinity has provided those anxious to prove Clausewitz's continuing relevance with plenty of food for thought. Many of these interpretations go far beyond what the text will bear, but such efforts are in part justified by Clausewitz's use of the word *mehr*, or 'mainly', when he links the passions to the people, the play of probability to the army, and the role of reason to the government. The qualification in the adverb allows for the possibility that the people can be rational, the army passionate, the government concerned with the play of probability and chance, and so on. Above all, he reintroduces the possibility that war can be elemental, rather than instrumental.

Clausewitz clearly says a great deal elsewhere in *On War* about the characteristics which he associates with the army, and a reasonable amount about the government and its policies. He seems to say less about passion or about the people who express it, and yet this is the element that has become central to the argument that future conflicts will not be fought by symmetrical armies within a European state system shaped by the balance of power – the wars which Clausewitz himself largely experienced and whose analysis dominated his writings – but will instead be waged by insurgents and non-state actors, using terrorism and ambush, dispersing rather than concentrating to fight.

Clausewitz regarded primitive peoples as possessed of a warlike spirit far greater than that of civilized peoples. Although he referred to Marathas, Tatars and Turks only in passing, he described Asia as a continent where 'a state of war is virtually permanent'.[64] One of the consequences of civilization was the loss of these warrior-like qualities, with the result that nations – like Prussia between 1763 and 1806 – became progressively less bold. Individual military genius, a quality not found in primitive societies, offset this decline in collective courage. Clausewitz thought that the

Russian general, Alexander Suvorov, was not up to the conduct of war which employed mass armies in developed countries because he had honed his skills fighting the Turks, a 'half-civilized people', whose wars were 'partial undertakings which achieved their effects as the sum of their parts rather than through their cohesion'.[65] Although dismissive of international law in moderating war, he did conclude that wars between civilized societies were less cruel and destructive than wars between savages: 'Savage peoples are ruled by passion, civilized peoples by the mind.'[66] Policy, being associated in the Clausewitzian trinity with reason, therefore had a greater field of influence within wars between civilized states. The implication here was that people were either passionately involved in war, but that in such wars policy and reason were marginalized, or that people were marginal and policy and reason dominant. But having suggested that peoples were not part of war's political dynamic, Clausewitz corrected himself. 'When whole communities go to war – whole peoples, and especially civilized peoples – the reason always lies in some political situation, and the occasion is always due to some political object [*Motiv*, not *Zweck*].'[67]

Even civilized peoples could be fired with passionate hatred, so combining depth of feeling and rationality. The main lesson of the French Revolution was that a people that was both civilized and passionate, and so politically aware, could create an army that was superior to the regular armies on which most of *On War*'s analysis focused.

Writing on the character of contemporary warfare in Book 3, chapter 17, Clausewitz reviewed the events of the later Napoleonic wars to show the 'enormous contribution the heart and temper of a nation can make to the sum total of its politics, war potential, and fighting strength'.[68] One of the examples to illustrate this triad – itself an anticipation of the trinity of Book 1, chapter 1 – was Prussia. After the treaty of Tilsit, Clausewitz and Gneisenau, inspired by the examples of Spain and Tyrol, had planned a national insurrection, intending to turn the idea of the nation in arms against France itself. In 1811, Clausewitz had filed a report on Silesia as the possible theatre for such a war,[69] and in 1813 the formation of the Landwehr had fulfilled the hopes of both of them for a popular rising. 'Prussia taught us in 1813', Clausewitz wrote in Book 3, 'that rapid efforts can increase an army's strength six times if we make use of a militia, and, what is more, that the militia can fight as well in foreign countries as at home.'[70] Advocating its retention after the peace, Clausewitz reminded Prussia that the Landwehr was superior in organization to the regular army it had possessed in the eighteenth century, precisely because it touched the entire people, infusing them with a warlike spirit, and enabling 'the element of war' to operate 'with all its raw natural power'.[71]

Despite his use of the epithet 'rapid' in his description of the events of 1813, Clausewitz was clear that a nation in arms could not be improvised, precisely because of the implicit contradiction between the peacetime avocations of civilized nations and the demands for boldness in war. France relied increasingly on long-service soldiers and foreign contingents during the course of the Napoleonic wars, and the result was that Napoleon had had to attack into Belgium in 1815, precisely because he could not reckon on enjoying any of the inherent benefits which popular passion gave to the defence. After its defeat at Waterloo, the French army – although falling back across its own country – was unsupported by the people: Clausewitz likened it to an army in a foreign land.[72]

Public opinion, already highlighted in his 1804 notes as an object in war, was identified as lying outside the army and independent of it. But, in the event of an invasion, the people might provide supplies and intelligence, while depriving the attacker of both. Their participation might even become active. Insurrectionary warfare, lauded by Clausewitz in 1809 in the light of events in Spain, showed how the spirit of the people could overcome the virtues of the regular army. Guerrillas were particularly effective in mountains and forests, geographical conditions which forced a regular army to disperse, so forfeiting its advantages of command and thus of military genius. Regulars preferred to fight in open country and seek battle; guerrillas spurned both. The value of insurrectionary or partisan war (Clausewitz used both titles) therefore lay within the relationship that most interested him, that between tactics and strategy. What partisans lacked in tactical effectiveness they gained through strategy. By avoiding battle they forced the enemy to disperse; the longer his line of communications, the more the opportunity for harassment and surprise. Thus they acted across the links between a field army and the theatre of war in which it was operating.[73]

Clausewitz refused to address the revolutionary implications of arming the people, rating the value of their contribution to the idea of national defence as more important than the consequences for domestic order. But this does not mean that in highlighting guerrilla war's role in linking tactics and strategy, Clausewitz neglected its contribution to the relationship between strategy and policy. Book 6, chapter 26, which was devoted to popular insurrection against an invader, is often read as demonstrating on the one hand Clausewitz's interest in the phenomenon and on the other his limited appreciation of its value. Because he saw it as ancillary to 'symmetrical' war between armies, he failed, or so the argument runs, to anticipate its potential to become free-standing in the way in which Martin van Creveld did in 1991. However, Clausewitz makes clear at the very beginning of the chapter that he was dealing with something that was both new in war and had the potential to become much bigger: 'A people's war in civilized Europe is a phenomenon of the nineteenth century.'[74]

'This sort of warfare', he wrote, 'is not as yet very common', and those who 'have been able to observe it for any length of time have not yet reported enough about it'.[75] The question that this remark prompts is whether Clausewitz himself intended to fill the gap in the literature even more fully than he did. The unfinished note on the manuscript of *On War* makes clear that Clausewitz saw his book at that stage as concerned with major war only.[76] He therefore recognized 'small war' as a subject worthy of separate study, and one possible implication is that, if he had lived longer, he himself might have undertaken such a work. This hypothesis rests on more than unsubstantiated speculation.

When Clausewitz joined the army in 1792, 'small war' carried very precise connotations. It encompassed the forms of fighting that took place away from the main battlefield, such as the protection of supplies, the harrying of outposts, and the collecting of intelligence. These responsibilities required select troops who were more reliable than the average soldier of the line, given the opportunities for desertion that detached duty presented, and who also showed more initiative and were probably better educated. In the wars on Europe's frontiers and in America, light cavalry and light infantry did more than screen the movements of the army's main body; they increasingly conducted a form of war that was independent and self-contained. Tactical flexibility, especially if it was elevated to strategic independence, carried implications for the democratization of an army which did not appeal to Frederick the Great or the more traditional officers of the Prussian army, but for those in the military reform movement it was the corollary of the political and social changes which armies were undergoing.

In 1810 Scharnhorst, who was planning popular resistance as the basis for Prussia to fight France, gave Clausewitz the task of lecturing on small war at the war school. Clausewitz's lecture notes constitute a sizeable body of work. His method was much more historical than abstract. He told his audience that too much recent writing lacked an understanding of war as it really was, and advised them to spurn 'the assimilation of rules by memory'.[77] He taught by way of case studies, including his own experience in 1793–4, whilst disarmingly acknowledging how limited it was. His principal references, and the reading he recommended to his students, were the works of Johann von Ewald and Andreas Emmerich, both Hessians who had served in the Seven Years War and in the American War of Independence.

At one level, therefore, Clausewitz was concerned to repeat the orthodoxies relating to small war as it had been understood in the eighteenth century. In part it was exactly what its title said it was – small because it involved fewer combatants. 'The strategy of small war is an area of tactics', he said; therefore the tactics of small war were also part of tactics, 'and so the whole of small war falls into tactics'.[78] The first part of his course covered outposts, and was consequently linked directly to the operations of major war, but the second dealt with partisans or the work of independent detachments. Even here, however, he reined in any inclination to see small war as a free-standing entity. When describing the role of partisans in pursuing a retreating enemy, he acknowledged that the implications of such action were strategic but concluded that in that case it no longer belonged in the realm of small war. The lectures were determinedly focused – like so much else that he wrote at this stage of his career – on tactical practice and therefore were, by his own lights, more susceptible to method than his condemnation of other theorists allowed for. His aim, he said, was to establish rules, albeit ones which were comprehensible and useable, and based on real events.[79]

The study of small war in the late eighteenth century was, however, also predicated on the assumption that it was a school of instruction for future commanders: indeed, that belief presumably underpinned the attention given to it at the Berlin war school in 1810. Clausewitz began his course by distinguishing it from the duties of the General Staff, which belonged to major war and were, in his word, mechanical. Small war was a matter of art and judgement, requiring cunning, flexibility and foresight: Clausewitz spoke of the 'free play of the spirit', using the same word, *Geist*, that he would later use of military genius.[80] Moreover, his examples did not stop short in 1794, but included references to the 'civil war' (his title) waged by French counter-revolutionaries in the Vendée against the Paris government in the mid-1790s, and the guerrilla wars conducted by the peoples of Tyrol and Spain – 'nations in arms' as he called them – against Napoleon in 1807–9.[81]

The latter proved inspirational for many German

nationalists, and Clausewitz's papers include a synopsis of the Peninsular War up until 1811. Here the tactics of small war acquired strategic and even political ends, and tied in with Clausewitz's preparations for anti-French resistance in Silesia. Ferdinand von Schill, who sustained partisan war against the French after the battle of Jena until his death in 1809, impressed both Clausewitz and Gneisenau. Schill had used the support of the local population to supply and hide his men, and Scharnhorst anticipated the formation of a home defence force which would wear no uniforms, would launch surprise attacks, and then melt back into the civilian community. These concepts underpinned the third of Clausewitz's political manifestos of February 1812, the document in which the tactical details of the war school lectures were fused with a Fichtean vision of national liberation. Calling for a levée en masse of the entire population aged eighteen to sixty, it argued that an insurgency could grow into a general war, in other words that small war could become a major war. Clausewitz acknowledged that such a conflict would be cruel, that 'the world trembles at the idea of a war of the people because it is more bloody than any other, that it seldom occurs without scenes of horror'. But, he asked, 'whose fault is that? Is it not the fault of those who drive others to the depths of desperation? They, not those on whom it has been forced, are to blame for its terrible consequences.'[82] Small war, derived from eighteenth-century tactical precepts but employing terror and atrocities, coalesced with the idea of existential war.

Book 6, chapter 26, embraces this possibility, that wars of the future would be waged by a politically aware, passionate people, fighting for the independence of their nation, and not ready to accept the verdict of the battlefield. They would broaden and intensify 'the whole ferment which we call war'. A people's war (Clausewitz used the word *Volkskrieg*) was 'a consequence of the way in which in our day the elemental violence of war has burst its old artificial barriers'.[83] Its methods would be those of small war, 'nebulous and elusive; its resistance should never materialize as a concrete body, otherwise the enemy can direct sufficient force at its core, crush it, and take many prisoners'. But there would still be times when the people would have to concentrate, when 'the fog must thicken and form a dark and menacing cloud out of which a bolt of lightning may strike at any time'.[84]

Typically, for this stage of his writing, Clausewitz, having set up a proposition, advanced its counter. Such concentrations were more likely to be on the flanks of the enemy army, and this in turn implied a theatre of war where time and space were sufficiently extensive to force the enemy army to disperse, thus enhancing the opportunities for the partisans. Only in Russia did he deem the geographical conditions sufficiently appropriate for a national insurrection to achieve a crisis without the involvement of regular forces. Although Clausewitz called this insight realism, in fact it marked the consequence of reality's interplay with theory. Neither Prussia after 1806 nor France in 1814 had embraced a war of national liberation.

Clausewitz could not therefore elevate the idea of a *Volkskrieg* to a universal model for the future, and indeed he would have looked one-dimensional and incoherent even today had he done so. But as the peroration to chapter 26 revealed, with its summons to existential war, and its reflection of the much more intense realities of 1812 and 1813, Clausewitz recognized that political necessity could in practice override military common sense. The crisis in his thinking which his undated note and the note of 1827 reveal was prompted in part by his awareness that there was much more to war than 'major war', and that might be more true, not less so, in the future. Clausewitz's understanding of the nature of war anticipated that its three elements, the trinity, could radically change its character. His theory allowed for the possibility of 'new wars' to a much greater extent than Martin van Creveld and Mary Kaldor have recognized.

CONCLUSION

On War is a book about war in the present and the immediate past – both of them Clausewitz's, not ours. It is not overtly a book about the future of war. Yet this is how it is often read, and not without reason. Clausewitz's core problem, even if largely implicit, was the likely shape of wars to come. In 1827, using the past as the basis for his judgement, he decided that there were two sorts of war: wars of observation and wars of decision. Only rarely did he permit himself prognostication as to which would prevail in the future. Moreover, he was not consistent in what he said. In Book 6, chapter 28, he wrote that, 'One may predict that most wars will tend to revert to wars of observation.'[1] From the short-term perspective of, say, 1850, that looked to have been a reasonable expectation: during the revolutions that swept Europe in 1830 and 1848 armies watched the antics of neighbouring states more often than they intervened in them. But a hundred years later, in 1950, Clausewitz's conclusion in Book 8, chapter 3B, would look more prescient. Having reviewed the history of war up until Napoleon, when 'war, untrammelled by any conventional restraints, had broken loose in all its elemental fury', he asked himself the logical question: 'Will this be the case in the future?' 'From now on will every war in Europe be waged with the full resources of the state, and therefore have to be fought only over major issues that affect the people?' He refused to give a straight answer, but, ever the realist, he went on to acknowledge that 'once barriers – which in a sense consist only in man's ignorance of what is possible – are torn down, they are not so easily put up again'.[2]

Clausewitz's reluctance to be dogmatic on the shape of future war highlights an extraordinary gap in his perception of war's nature. He saw strategy as dependent on tactics. His reflections on tactics, which mirrored the debates of the day, were not particularly original. Should infantry be deployed in lines to maximize their firepower, or in columns for shock and mobility? Given the value of field artillery's firepower, how many guns could an army comfortably accommodate without jeopardizing its own mobility? What was the correct use of cavalry when it was vulnerable to the fire even of smoothbore weapons but remained vital to the exploitation of battlefield success?[3] In answering these questions, he inclined to favour the effects of firepower over shock. And yet, despite his own interests in mechanics and the physical sciences, he never explored the consequences of technological change either for firepower specifically or for war more generally. His discussion in Book 5, chapter 4, of how the three arms should be balanced in the composition of an army, dwelt on terrain more than technology as the determinant of the relative numbers of cavalry and artillery. By 1871, the principles of breech-loading and rifling were being applied both to the infantryman's firearm and to artillery; the railway had transformed the movements and supply of armies; and the telegraph had changed for ever the general's relationship to his political masters. Following his own logic, greater fire effect had the potential to alter tactics and therefore strategy, but when Clausewitz ruminated on the future of war, he saw change solely in social and political terms. There could be no more graphic indication of the influence of his own times: war in the age of Napoleon was transformed not by technology, but by social and political revolution.

Picking holes in *On War* is an easy game: it is massively Eurocentric; there is nothing on navies and little on economics. Written in an era when sovereign states enjoyed an unfettered right to resort to war, it neglected international law to an extent unacceptable since 1945. Moreover, Clausewitz contradicts himself, as this book has shown repeatedly. But that is also *On War*'s strength, its very essence and the reason for its longevity. It is a work in progress. Its unfinished nature should be a source not of frustration but of joy. Its author never stopped asking questions – not simply of his own conclusions but also of the methods by which he had reached them. The extraordinary fertility of his mind means that any attempt to seek uniformity and consistency in his arguments runs the risk of doing violence to their insights. Every generation has tended to look at what Clausewitz wrote in the light of its own preoccupations, but in using his thoughts in this way is always in danger of treating the text selectively. That in itself is neither illegitimate nor inappropriate, but by the same token no one school can claim the monopoly of wisdom in its interpretation of Clausewitz's work. Freezing his thought at any stage of its development, even the allegedly sacrosanct one represented by Book 1, chapter 1, creates the danger both that the very richness of the author's mind will be lost, and that *On War* itself will be consigned to premature oblivion.

The introduction showed the frequency with which Clausewitz has been declared dead, not just since 1990, but also after 1918 and 1945. The chapters which followed demonstrated how many axioms derived from *On War* can be countered by others, also drawn from the same text. Clausewitz knew full well that policy can expand war as well as limit it; that absolute war can approach a reality as well as form a theoretical concept; and that the people are as central to war as are the government and army. Clausewitz's maturation was marked not by his making up his mind on these issues, but by his growing commitment to the methodology of dialectics. Clausewitz himself – to commit the very sin of selective quotation – gave the best riposte to those who seek to pigeon-hole him: war, he said, was 'a true chameleon, because it adapts its nature to meet each case'.[4] But then, of course, he went on to qualify the statement.

NOTES

Introduction

1 Colin Powell, with Joseph Persico, *My American Journey*, New York, Random House, 1995, pp. 207–8.

2 Harry G. Summers, Jr., *On Strategy: A critical analysis of the Vietnam war*, Novato, CA, Presidio, 1981, pp. 4, 6.

3 Christopher Bassford, *Clausewitz in English*, New York, Oxford University Press, 1994, p. 204.

4 Russell Weigley, 'The American military and the principle of civilian control from McClellan to Powell', *Journal of Military History*, 57, 5 (special issue), 1993, p. 29.

5 Tommy Franks, with Malcolm McConnell, *American Soldier*, New York, Regan Books, 2004, p. 165.

6 Clausewitz, *Ausgewählte militärische Schriften*, Berlin, Militärverlag der deutschen Demokratischen Republik, 1981, edited by Gerhard Förster and Dorothea Schmidt, p. 372.

7 Clausewitz, 'Der Feldzug von 1796 in Italien', in *Sämtliche Schriften 'Vom Kriege'*, Mundus, 1999, Band 2, p. 17.

8 Quoted by Ami-Jacques Rapin, *Jomini et la stratégie: une approche historique de l'oeuvre*, Lausanne, Payot, 2002, p. 205.

9 Ulrich Marwedel, *Carl von Clausewitz. Persönlichkeit und*

Wirkungsgeschichte seiner Werkes bis 1918, Boppard am Rhein, Harald Boldt, 1978, p. 117.

10 Gerhard Ritter, *The Sword and the Scepter: The problem of militarism in Germany*, 4 vols, Coral Gables, Florida, University of Miami Press, 1969–72, vol. I, pp. 194–5.

11 Ibid., vol. I, p. 195.

12 Daniel J. Hughes (ed.), *Moltke on the Art of War: Selected writings*, Novato, CA, Presidio, 1993, p. 47.

13 G. G. [Gilbert], *Essais de critique militaire*, Paris, *La Nouvelle Revue*, 1890, p. 20; from an article first published in *La Nouvelle Revue* in 1887.

14 Ferdinand Foch, *The Principles of War*, London, Chapman and Hall, 1918; first published in France, 1903, pp. 4–5, 42.

15 Basil Liddell Hart, *Foch: The Man of Orleans*, London, Eyre and Spottiswoode, 1931, p. 21.

16 Basil Liddell Hart, *The Ghost of Napoleon*, London, Faber & Faber, 1933, p. 122.

17 Erich Ludendorff, *The Nation at War*, London, Hutchinson, n.d., p. 24.

18 Ibid., p. 23.

19 Hans-Adolf Jacobsen, *Karl Haushofer – Leben und Werk*, 2 vols, Boppard am Rhein, Harald Boldt, 1979, p. 376.

20 Clausewitz, *Vom Kriege*, abridged edition edited by Friedrich von Cochenhausen, Leipzig, Insel, 1937, p. 5.

21 Bernard Semmel (ed.), *Marxism and the Science of War*, Oxford, Oxford University Press, 1981, p. 66. The German word is *Witz*, which Semmel translates as 'brilliance'.

22 Ibid., p. 69.

23 Olaf Rose, *Carl von Clausewitz. Wirkungsgeschichte seines*

Werkes Russland und der Sowjetunion 1836–1991, Munich, Oldenbourg, 1995, p. 205.

24 David Holloway, *The Soviet Union and the Arms Race*, New Haven, Yale University Press, 1983, p. 165.

25 Ritter originally published these views in 1943 in the *Historisches Zeitschrift*, see P. M. Baldwin, 'Clausewitz in Nazi Germany', *Journal of Contemporary History*, XVI (1981), p. 19.

26 Michael Mandelbaum, *The Nuclear Question: The United States and nuclear weapons 1946–1976*, Cambridge, Cambridge University Press, 1979, pp. 3–4.

27 Stewart L. Murray, *The Reality of War: An introduction to 'Clausewitz'*, London, Hugh Rees, 1909, p. 10.

Chapter 1

1 *On War*, p. 61. Published by Maria von Clausewitz in her Introduction to the original edition, and as a separate note by Howard and Paret.

2 Karl Linnebach (ed.), *Karl u. Marie von Clausewitz. Ein Lebensbild in Briefen und Tagebuchblättern*, Berlin, Martin Warneck, 1917, p. 110.

3 Ibid., p. 138.

4 Ibid., p. 135.

5 *On War*. 8, 3B, Jolles, p. 584.

6 Or he said he was: the church register says 1 July. See Gerhard Förster, *Carl von Clausewitz*, Berlin, Militärverlag der deutschen Demokratischen Republik, 1983, p. 1.

7 *On War*, p. 66.

8 Hans Rothfels, *Carl von Clausewitz. Politik und Krieg*, Berlin, Dümmler, 1920; new edition, Bonn, Dümmler, 1980, p. 102.

9 Clausewitz, *Vom Kriege*, Book 6, chapter 23, p. 665; this is omitted or moderated in all English translations.

10 Linnebach, *Karl u. Marie Clausewitz*, p. 96.

11 Ibid., p. 83. The reference is to a fictional character in Friedrich Schiller's trilogy, *Wallenstein* (1798–9); Piccolomini is the spokesman of Schiller's philosophical and moral position, reflecting the influence of Kant.

12 Clausewitz, *Preussen in seiner grossen Katastrophe*, first published 1880; reprinted, Vienna, Karolinger, 2001, p. 19.

13 Comte de Guibert, *A General Essay on Tactics*, 2 vols, London, 1781, vol. I, p. viii. For Clausewitz's use of it, see Clausewitz, *Schriften-Aufsätze-Studien-Briefe*, 2 vols, Göttingen, Vandenhoeck & Ruprecht, 1966–90, edited by Werner Hahlweg, vol. 1, pp. 710–11.

14 *On War*, 6, 30, p. 515.

15 Ibid., 6, 30, p. 518.

16 Scharnhorst, 'Entwicklung der allgemeinen Ursachen des Glücks der Franzosen in dem Revolutionskriege und insbesondere in dem Feldzüge von 1794', Gerhard von Scharnhorst, *Ausgewählte militärische Schriften*, hg. Hansjürgen Usczeck and Christa Gudzent, Berlin, Militärverlag der deutschen Demokratischen Republik, 1986, p. 105.

17 Linnebach, *Karl u. Maria Clausewitz*, p. 128.

18 Ibid., p. 85. Clausewitz used the word 'Geist', which means both intellect and spirit; the problems of translating this word, so important to Clausewitz and used by him so often, are discussed below, pp. 92–4, 126.

19 Clausewitz, *Strategie aus dem Jahr 1804 mit Zusätzen von 1808 und 1809*, Hamburg, Hanseatische Verlagsanstalt, 1937, edited by Eberhard Kessel, p. 56.

20 'Considérations sur la manière de faire la guerre à la France' in Clausewitz, *Schriften*, edited by Werner Hahlweg, vol. I, pp. 58–63.

21 Clausewitz, *Preussen in seiner grossen Katastrophe*, pp. 9, 53, 72–3, 78.

22 Linnebach, *Karl u. Maria Clausewitz*, p. 59.

23 Clausewitz, *Preussen in seiner grossen Katastrophe*, p. 20.

24 Linnebach, *Karl u. Maria Clausewitz*, p. 65.

25 Clausewitz, 'Historische Briefe über die grossen Kriegereignisse im Oktober 1806' in Clausewitz, *Ausgewählte militärische Schriften*, Berlin, Militäverlag der deutschen Demokratischen Republik, 1981, edited by Gerhard Förster and Dorothea Schmidt, p. 73.

26 Ibid., p. 75.

27 Linnebach, *Karl u. Maria Clausewitz*, p. 71.

28 Werner Hahlweg, *Clausewitz. Soldat-Politiker-Denker*, Göttingen, Musterschmidt-Verlag, 1969, p. 33.

29 Clausewitz to Gneisenau, 17 June 1811, in Clausewitz, *Schriften*, edited by Hahlweg, p. 645; see *On War*, 2, p. 133.

30 Linnebach, *Karl u. Maria Clausewitz*, p. 226.

31 Clausewitz, *Schriften*, edited by Hahlweg, vol. 1, pp. 66–90, here pp. 79, 81, 89.

32 Ibid., p. 638.

33 Clausewitz, *Historical and Political Writings*, Princeton, Princeton University Press, 1992, edited and translated by Peter Paret and Daniel Moran, p. 290; for the full and annotated text, see Clausewitz, *Schriften*, vol. 1, pp. 682–750. Hahlweg calls these documents collectively 'Bekenntnisdenkschrift', which could be translated as a 'statement of confession'; Paret and Moran settle for

'political declaration'; Clausewitz himself gave them no title.

34 Adolf Hitler, *Mein Kampf*, London, Hurst & Blackett, 1939, pp. 544–5, 1938, pp. 759–61.

35 *On War*, 6, 26, p. 483.

36 Clausewitz, *Historical and Political Writings*, p. 300.

37 Clausewitz, *Strategie aus dem Jahr 1804*, p. 42.

38 Clausewitz, *Historical and Political Writings*, p. 201; see also Clausewitz, *The Campaign of 1812 in Russia*, first published 1843; reprinted New York, Da Capo, 1995, p. 252; *On War*, 8, 9, pp. 626–7.

39 Clausewitz, *Campaign of 1812*, p. 253.

40 Ibid., pp. 95–8, 253–5; *On War*, 3, 12, p. 208; 4, 12, p. 266; 5, 12, p. 323; 5, 14, p. 336; 6, 8, p. 385.

41 Clausewitz, *Campaign of 1812*, p. 14; *On War*, 8, 8, p. 615.

42 To Gneisenau, 7 November 1812, in Clausewitz, *Schriften*, edited by Hahlweg, vol. 2, p. 131.

43 Linnebach, *Karl u. Marie von Clausewitz*, p. 304.

44 Writing to Marie, 29 November 1812, in ibid., p. 305.

45 Clausewitz, *Ausgewählte militärische Schriften*, ed. Förster and Schmidt, p. 306.

46 On the two battles and their contexts, see T. C. W. Blanning, *The French Revolutionary Wars 1787–1802*, London, Arnold, 1996, and David Gates, *The Napoleonic Wars 1803–1815*, London, Arnold, 1997.

47 Clausewitz, *Ausgewählte Militärische Schriften.*, p. 256.

48 Linnebach, *Karl u. Marie von Clausewitz*, p. 341.

49 Ibid., p. 365.

50 Clausewitz, 'Our military institutions', in *Historical and Political Writings*, p. 317.

51 Clausewitz, 'On the political advantages and disadvantages

of the Prussian Landwehr', in *Historical and Political Writings*, p. 332.

52 Clausewitz, *Schriften*, edited by Hahlweg, vol. 2, pp. 592–3.

53 Linnebach, *Karl u. Marie von Clausewitz*, p. 447.

Chapter 2

1 Clausewitz, *Ausgewählte Briefe an Marie von Clausewitz und Gneisenau*, Berlin, Verlag der Nation, 1953, p. 264.

2 *On War* (Howard and Paret edition), p. 66.

3 Peter Paret, 'The genesis of *On War*', ibid., pp. 6–7.

4 Ibid., 5, 9, p. 313.

5 *On War*, p. 67.

6 *On War*, p. 70.

7 Clausewitz, *Schriften*, edited by Werner Hahlweg, vol. 2, pp. 625–7. See also Walther Malmsten Schering, *Die Kriegsphilosophie von Clausewitz*, Hamburg, Hanseatische Verlagsanstalt, 1935, pp. 24–6.

8 *On War*, 8, 9, p. 636.

9 *On War*, Jolles, pp. xxix–xxx.

10 Clausewitz, *Strategie aus dem Jahr 1804*, pp. 51–2.

11 *On War*, 6, 30, p. 515; 7, 22, p. 570; 8, 2, p. 580; 8, 3, p. 583; 8, 3, p. 592.

12 Peter Paret, *Clausewitz and the State*, Oxford, Oxford University Press, 1976, p. 330, suggests a chronology, which I have only partly followed. The dates suggested for the study of 1806 are contradicted by the introduction to the French edition of 1903, *Notes sur la Prusse dans sa grande catastrophe. 1806*, Paris, R. Chapelot, 1903, pp. 2–3.

13 Clausewitz, 'Die Feldzüge von 1799 in Italien und Schweiz', in *Sämtliche Schriften 'Vom Kriege'*, Band 2, p. 317.

14 Clausewitz, *Principles of War*, London, John Lane, The Bodley Head, 1943, edited by Hans W. Gatzke, p. 54.

15 Andreas Herberg-Rothe, *Das Rätsel Clausewitz*, Munich, Wilhelm Fink, 2001, pp. 27–49.

16 Azar Gat, *The Origins of Military Thought from the Enlightenment to Clausewitz*, Oxford, Oxford University Press, 1989, pp. 199–252.

17 Clausewitz, *Two Letters on Strategy*, edited and translated by Peter Paret and Daniel Moran, US Army War College, 1984; see also Peter Paret, *Understanding War*, Princeton, Princeton University Press, 1992, pp. 123–9.

18 *On War*, 6, 8, p. 389; Howard and Paret translate this passage as though it refers to the whole work, and thus minimize the innovatory point of the observation, but Clausewitz referred to '*unseres Buches*', which could refer specifically to Book 6.

19 *On War*, p. 62.

20 This discussion is informed by the outlines for the book contained in Clausewitz, *Schriften*, edited by Hahlweg, vol. 2, pp. 623–716, and especially pp. 675–80, an outline for Book 8.

21 *On War*, 2, 2, p. 136; also 2, 5, pp. 168–9.

22 *On War*, 4, 11 and 12 (Graham edition), 1, pp. 289, 292. Howard and Paret, here and elsewhere in this book, elect not to translate '*System*' as system.

23 *On War*, 3, 14; this is an adapted version of Graham, vol. I, p. 221, which gets nearer to the original German than any other translation.

24 *On War*, 4, 12, p. 267; 5, 7, p. 304; 5, 9, p. 312; 5, 13, p. 328; 5, 15, p. 342; 5, 17, p. 348; 5, 18, p. 353; 6, 2, p. 360; 6, 4, p. 368; 6, 18, pp. 433–5.

25 Ibid., 5, 17, p. 348.
26 Ibid., 4, 4, p. 234; 4, 9, p. 250; 4, 10, p. 253.
27 Ibid., 5, 2, p. 280.
28 Because Howard and Paret frequently prefer to translate 'philosophisch' as scientific, the point is lost in this translation; Clausewitz eschews '*wissenschaftlich*', which is what their rendering implies. See Werner Hahlweg, 'Philosophie und Theorie bei Clausewitz' in Eberhard Wagemann and Joachim Niemeyer (eds), *Freiheit ohne Krieg?*, Bonn, Dümmler 1980.
29 *On War*, p. 63.
30 Herberg-Rothe, *Das Rätsel Clausewitz*, pp. 92–3.
31 Ibid., pp. 107–21; Paret, *Clausewitz and the State*, p. 316; Raymond Aron, *Penser la guerre, Clausewitz*, 2 vols, Paris, Gallimard, 1976, vol. 1, pp. 360–5; Gat, *Origins of Military Thought*, pp. 230–35.
32 Linnebach, *Karl u. Marie von Clausewitz*, pp. 154–5.
33 Clausewitz, *Historical and Political Writings*, p. 282.
34 Clausewitz, *Strategie aus dem Jahr 1804*, pp. 40–41, 76; see also *On War*, 2, 2, p. 145.
35 Rothfels, *Carl von Clausewitz*, p. 107; see also pp. 130–31.
36 Werner Hahlweg, *Clausewitz. Soldat-Politiker-Denker*, p. 37.
37 He does use it in Book 1, chapter 1, para 3, suggesting that he perhaps planned to return to it as the more rational Clausewitz manifested himself towards the end of his life, but the context is not specifically to do with the attributes of the commander.
38 Clausewitz, *Geist und Tat*, Stuttgart, Alfred Kröner, 1941, edited by Walther Malmsten Schering, pp. 153–78; see Gat, *Origins of Military Thought*, pp. 175–84.

39 Hahlweg, *Clausewitz*, p. 34.
40 *On War*, 2, 3, p. 149.
41 Ibid., 2, 5, p. 156; also 8, 1, p. 578.
42 Ibid., 2, 4, p. 152; also 8, 1, p. 578.
43 Ibid., 2, 2, p. 141.
44 Ibid., 6, 8, p. 388.
45 Ibid., 1, 7, p. 120.
46 Clausewitz, *Strategie aus dem Jahr 1804*, p. 66.
47 Clausewitz, *Principles of War*, pp. 54–5.
48 *On War*, 6, 6, p. 374; for what has gone before, see 2, 2, p. 144; 2, 4, p. 154; 2, 6, p. 171; 6, 30, p. 506, p. 517 and p. 519; 8, 2, p. 579.
49 Ibid., 4, 11, p. 261.
50 Ibid., 2, 1, p. 127.
51 Ibid., 2, 5, p. 165; 2, 6, p. 173; 6, 10, pp. 398–9; 6, 30, p. 506; see also the discussion of sources in Clausewitz, 'Die Feldzüge von 1799 in Italien und der Schweiz', in *Sämtliche Schriften 'Vom Kriege'*, Band 2.
52 Ibid., 2, 6, p. 174; 5, 6, p. 297; 5, 14, p. 330; 6, 2, pp. 361–2; 6, 30, p. 514; 7, 13–14, pp. 542–3; 8, 3, p. 589; see also Rudolf von Caemmerer, *Clausewitz*, Berlin, Oldenburg, 1905, p. 76.
53 Ibid., 2, 2, p. 141; 2, 5, p. 168.
54 Ibid., 6, 30, pp. 516–17; see also 3, 16, p. 218; 4, 3, p. 228.
55 Ibid., 7, 20, p. 562; 5, 2, p. 281.
56 Ibid., 1, 2, p. 98.

Chapter 3

1 Clausewitz, *Vom Kriege*, Berlin, Dümmler, 1952, pp. 73, 80.
2 *On War*, 3, 1, p. 177; see also 3, 10, p. 202; 6, 30, p. 509.

3 Ibid., 2, 2, p. 143; 3, 6, p. 191; 3, 8, p. 194; 6, 1, p. 358; 6, 3, p. 363; see also Clausewitz, 'Die Feldzüge von 1799', in *Sämtliche Schriften 'Vom Kriege'*, Band 2, p. 373.

4 Clausewitz, *Schriften*, edited by Werner Hahlweg, vol. 2, p. 327.

5 *On War*, 6, 4, p. 368; see also 5, 5, p. 293; 7, 19, p. 557.

6 Ibid., 7, 19, p. 577.

7 Ibid., 2, 2, p. 143. Clausewitz's confused use of *Zweck* is indicative of the gestatory status of his thoughts in Book 2. In *On War*, 2, 2, Howard and Paret, p. 146, anticipate what followed later in the text by inserting words like 'policies', which is how they interpreted *Richtungen*.

8 Clausewitz, *Schriften*, edited by Hahlweg, vol. 1, p. 645; see also Clausewitz, *De la revolution à la Restauration: Écrits et Lettres*, Paris, Gallimard, 1976, edited by Marie-Louise Steinhauser, pp. 66–87, especially p. 78; Clausewitz, *Strategie aus dem Jahr 1804*, pp. 62, 79.

9 *On War*, 4, 12, p. 267; for previous points see 5, 7, p. 302; 7, 18, pp. 555–6.

10 Ibid., 2, 1, p. 132.

11 These points are scattered throughout Book 6, but see especially 8, p. 380; 9, p. 390; 12, pp. 404–7; 15, p. 417; 16, p. 423; as well as 5, 18, p. 353; 7, 2, p. 525.

12 Ibid., 3, 13, p. 211; see also 3, 9, pp. 198–9; 3, 12, pp. 206–12; see Clausewitz, 'Die Feldzüge von 1799', in *Sämtliche Schriften 'Vom Kriege'*, 1999, Band 2, pp. 548–50.

13 Clausewitz, 'Strategische Übersicht des Feldzugs von 1815', paras 12, 32, 45, in *Sämtliche Schriften 'Vom Kriege'*, 1999, Band 3, pp. 330, 357–64, 391–3.

14 *On War*, 4, 7, p. 242.

15 Clausewitz, 'Strategische Übersicht des Feldzugs von 1815', para 48, pp. 397–412; see also para 32, and Clausewitz, *Campaign of 1812*, p. 166; Clausewitz, *Historical and Political Writings*, p. 147.

16 *On War*, 4, 4, p. 233; see also 4, 7, p. 242; 6, 2, p. 360; 6, 4, pp. 367–8; 7, 7, p. 530.

17 Ibid., 5, 6, pp. 299–300; 5, 7, p. 304; 5, 16, pp. 346–7; 6, 4, pp. 367–8; 6, 24, pp. 460–66; 6, 28, pp. 492–4; 7, 7, p. 530; 7, 22, p. 568; Clausewitz, 'Die Feldzüge von 1799', p. 770.

18 Clausewitz, 'Der Feldzug von 1796 in Italien', in *Sämtliche Schriften 'Vom Kriege'*, Band 2, p. 71.

19 Ibid., 3, 13, p. 211; 4, 2, p. 226; 4, 3, p. 228; 6, 8, p. 386.

20 Clausewitz, *Schriften*, edited by Hahlweg, vol. 1, p. 645.

21 *On War*, 2, 4, pp. 152–3.

22 Clausewitz, *Strategie aus dem Jahr 1804*, p. 40.

23 A. H. Jomini, *Summary of the Art of War*, Philadelphia, J. B. Lippincott, 1862, translated by G. H. Mendell and W. P. Craighill, p. 178.

24 *On War*, 6, 30, p. 514.

25 *On War*, 7, 13, p. 541; see also 4, 4, p. 230; 6, 8, pp. 385–6; 4, 3, p. 228.

26 Clausewitz, 'Feldzug von 1815', para 22, pp. 341–3.

27 *On War*, 4, 4, p. 230.

28 Ibid., 5, 14, p. 336.

29 Clausewitz, *Principles of War*, pp. 42–3, 53; but see the original German, IV, para 7, printed as an appendix to Clausewitz, *Vom Kriege*, edited by Hahlweg, pp. 981–2.

30 *On War*, 5, 14, p. 338; see also 8, 9, pp. 622–3.

31 Ibid., 5, 3, p. 282.

32 Clausewitz, *Strategie aus dem Jahr 1804*, p. 41.

33 *On War*, 2, 2, p. 136, Howard and Paret translate *geistigen Grössen* as 'moral factors', which in this case seems to miss the essence of Clausewitz's intent. See also Walther Malmsten Schering, *Die Kriegsphilosophie von Clausewitz*, pp. 16–17.
34 *On War*, 4, 4, p. 231; for what has gone before see 1, 3, p. 101; 2, 2, pp. 136–8; 3, 3, pp. 184–8; 7, 15, p. 545.
35 Ibid., 3, 6, p. 192. The English translation softens the force of this passage, especially when it revolves around the word *Volk*, conveying both people and nation. See also 5, 17, p. 350.
36 Ibid., 3, 6, p. 192.
37 Ibid., 2, 2, p. 146.
38 Ibid., 1, 3, p. 102.
39 Clausewitz, 'Feldzug von 1796 in Italien', in *Sämtliche Schriften 'Vom Kriege'*, Band 2, p. 71.
40 *On War*, 5, 3, pp. 283–4; see also 4, 4, p. 231; 4, 10, pp. 254–6; 7, 15, p. 545.
41 Ibid., 2, 2, p. 135; 3, 8, pp. 194–5.
42 Ibid., 5, 3, p. 283; see also 3, 12, p. 208; 6, 22, p. 570.
43 Ibid., 3, 11, p. 204; also 3, 8, pp. 195–6.
44 Ibid., 5, 2, p. 280; 5, 14, p. 338; 6, 25, p. 472; 6, 29, p. 499.
45 Ibid., 6, 27, p. 484. Howard and Paret, as is their wont, translate 'theatre of war' as 'theatre of operations'; I have amended their translation to conform with Clausewitz's choice of words. For later definitions of war plans, see 8, 2, p. 579; 8, 6B, p. 607.
46 Ibid., 8, 9, p. 619.
47 Ibid., 4, 11, Jolles, p. 211.
48 Ibid., 6, 27, p. 485.

49 Ibid., 6, 23, p. 459.

50 Ibid., 8, 4, Jolles, p. 586; see Clausewitz, 'Strategische Kritik des Feldzugs von 1814 in Frankreich', in *Sämtliche Schriften 'Vom Kriege'*, Band 3, pp. 240, 243; 'Strategische Übersicht des Feldzugs von 1815', para 56 in ibid., pp. 440 –7.

51 *On War*, 4, 11, p. 260.

52 Ibid., 1, 1, p. 81.

53 Ibid., 4, 1, p. 227.

54 Ibid., 4, 11, p. 258.

55 Ibid., 1, 2, p. 99.

56 Ibid., 4, 11, p. 259.

57 Ibid., 3, 12, p. 206; 4, 7, p. 241; see also Clausewitz, 'Die Feldzüge von 1799', p. 321.

58 Ibid., 4, 4, pp. 230–1.

59 Clausewitz, *Schriften*, edited by Hahlweg, vol. 2, p. 249.

60 *On War*, 8, 4, p. 599.

61 Ibid., 3, 11, p. 205.

62 Ibid., 5, 14, p. 338; see also 5, 13, p. 325.

63 Ibid., 1, 1, Jolles, p. 8.

64 Ibid., 4, 9, p. 248; 4, 10, p. 254; 4, 11, p. 258.

65 Ibid., 6, 28, p. 489.

66 See Clausewitz, *Vom Kriege*, 5, 3, p. 401; 5, 6, p. 422; 5, 8, p. 441; 6, 15, pp. 611–12; 6, 16, pp. 616–17; 6, 30, pp. 744–6; 7, 11, p. 793; 7, 16, pp. 808–9.

67 Ibid., 3, 1, p. 182; 4, 9, p. 250; 6, 8, p. 384; 6, 28, p. 489; 7, 6, p. 529.

68 Ibid., 8, 9, p. 626. Earlier in the same paragraph, Clausewitz uses the word *ersten*, which Howard and Paret translate as a 'single campaign', but I read as the 'first campaign'.

69 Ibid., 1, 1, p. 75.

70 *On War*, 2, 3, p. 149.
71 Clausewitz, *Schriften*, edited by Hahlweg, vol. 2, p. 250.
72 *On War*, 1, 3, p. 104.
73 Clausewitz, *Schriften*, edited by Hahlweg, vol. 2, pp. 249, 251.
74 Clausewitz, 'Die Feldzüge von 1799', p. 602; see also p. 790.

Chapter 4

1 Basil Liddell Hart, *The Ghost of Napoleon*, London, Faber & Faber, 1933, p. 120.
2 Peter Paret, *Clausewitz and the State*, Oxford, Oxford University Press, 1976, p. 367.
3 Clausewitz, *Strategie aus dem Jahr 1804 mit Zusätzen von 1808 und 1809*, Hamburg, Hanseatische Verlagsanstalt, 1937, introduction by Eberhard Kessel, p. 32.
4 Clausewitz, *Schriften*, edited by Werner Hahlweg, vol. 1, p. 300.
5 *On War*, 6, 15, pp. 419–20; see also 6, 16, p. 424; see also Clausewitz, 'Die Feldzüge von 1799', p. 585.
6 *On War*, 6, 17, p. 427.
7 Ibid., 5, 9, p. 313; see also 5, 13, p. 325.
8 Ibid., 6, 28, pp. 488–9; see also 6, 30, p. 501.
9 Ibid., 8, 2, Jolles, p. 570; by omitting certain words, especially *wirklichen* or 'real', Howard and Paret soften the force of this passage.
10 Ibid., 8, 3, Jolles, pp. 572–3. Clausewitz says that absolute war occurs '*wenig*', which Jolles accurately translates as 'little', but Howard and Paret, no doubt seeking consistency with Book 1, chapter 1, render as 'never'.
11 Ibid., 8, 3, Jolles, p. 574.

12 Ibid., 8, 3B, Jolles, pp. 583–4; see also 8, 6, Jolles, p. 601.
13 Clausewitz, *Schriften*, edited by Hahlweg, vol. 2, pp. 632–5.
14 *On War*, 1, 1, p. 86.
15 Ibid., 1, 1, p. 80, para 9; Howard and Paret confuse the issue by translating *Absoluten* as 'final'.
16 Paret, *Clausewitz and the State*, p. 124; Clausewitz, *Schriften*, edited by Hahlweg, vol. 1, p. 445; Clausewitz, *Principles of War*, London, John Lane, The Bodley Head, 1943, edited by Hans W. Gatzke, pp. 42, 50–51; Clausewitz's letter to Fichte, *Historical and Political Writings*, Princeton, Princeton University Press, 1992, p. 282. Compare these passages with *On War*, 1, 7, pp. 119–22.
17 Clausewitz, 'The campaign of 1812 in Russia', in *Historical and Political Writings*, pp. 165–6.
18 Clausewitz, *Schriften*, edited by Hahlweg, vol. 2, p. 250.
19 Clausewitz, *Principles of War*, pp. 43–8; see also Clausewitz, *Strategie aus dem Jahr 1804*, p. 18; Clausewitz, *Schriften*, edited by Hahlweg, vol. 1, pp. 741–3.
20 Clausewitz, 'Strategische Kritik des Feldzugs von 1814 im Frankreich', in *Sämtliche Schriften 'Vom Kriege'*, Band 3, pp. 238–9; *On War*, 6, 7, p. 377.
21 Clausewitz, *Strategie aus dem Jahr 1804*, pp. 46, 54, 63, 71; see also Clausewitz, *Principles of War*, p. 39.
22 *On War*, 6, 28, p. 488.
23 Clausewitz, 'Strategische Kritik des Feldzugs von 1814 im Frankreich', pp. 241, 253.
24 Clausewitz, *Schriften*, edited by Hahlweg, vol. 1, p. 300.
25 Clausewitz, 'Strategisches Kritik des Feldzugs von 1814 im Frankreich', pp. 247–8.

26 Clausewitz, *Schriften*, edited by Hahlweg, vol. 1, p. 747; see also Hans Rothfels, *Carl von Clausewitz. Politik und Krieg*, Berlin, Dümmler, 1920, p. 158.
27 *On War*, 3, 1, p. 178; see also 3, 13, p. 210. Howard and Paret translate *Verhältnissen des Staates* in the next paragraph as 'political conditions', which suggests that here Clausewitz might have meant domestic politics, an interpretation which I reject for Book 3.
28 Ibid., 3, 8, p. 196; 5, 3, p. 283; 5, 4, p. 287; 6, 2, p. 360.
29 Ibid., 4, 3, p. 227; see also 4, 8, p. 245.
30 Ibid., 6, 28, p. 494.
31 Ibid., 8, 6B, Jolles, p. 598.
32 Clausewitz, *Historical and Political Writings*, p. 245.
33 Ibid., pp. 243–4.
34 *On War*, 6, 6, pp. 373–4.
35 Ibid., 8, 3B, p. 590; see also 8, 6A, p. 603.
36 Ibid., 8, 5, p. 602, suggests the contrary by translating *inneren* as 'domestic' rather than 'intrinsic'.
37 Ibid., 8, 6B, pp. 606–7.
38 Clausewitz, *Historical and Political Writings*, p. 312.
39 Clausewitz, *Preussen in seiner grossen Katastrophe*, first published 1880; reprinted, Vienna, Karolinger, 2001, p. 12.
40 Clausewitz, 'Der Feldzüge von 1799', p. 784; see also Werner Hahlweg, *Clausewitz. Soldat-Politiker-Denker*, Göttingen, 1969, p. 57; Clausewitz, 'Feldzug von 1796', pp. 104, 158–9, 216.
41 *On War*, 6, 26, p. 483.
42 Ibid., 8, 9, p. 633.
43 Ibid., 1, 3, Jolles, p. 45; 2, 2, Jolles, pp. 81–2; in both passages Howard and Paret gloss the German text, with the result

that the political element is generalized and the specifically foreign policy context is diminished.

44 Ibid., 8, 6B, p. 608.

45 *On War*, 8, 3B, p. 592.

46 Ibid., 8, 3B, Jolles, p. 583.

47 Ibid., 8, 3B, p. 594.

48 Clausewitz, 'Strategische Kritik des Feldzugs von 1814 im Frankreich', p. 235.

49 *On War*, 8, 6B, p. 605; for the preceding points, see 5, 14, p. 330; 6, 8, pp. 387–8; 6, 30, p. 513; 8, 4, p. 600; 8, 6B, p. 610.

50 Ibid., 8, 6B, pp. 605–6. Howard and Paret translate *ganz Krieg* as 'total war', giving the text a twentieth-century spin that does violence to the surrounding debate which points up the contrast with 'half war'. Elsewhere in their translation they render *ganz Krieg* as 'whole war'.

51 Clausewitz to Gneisenau, 24 November 1827, in *Schriften*, edited by Hahlweg, vol. 2, p. 533.

52 Clausewitz, 'Strategischer Übersicht des Feldzugs von 1815' in *Sämtliche Schriften 'Vom Kriege'*, Band 3, p. 423.

53 *On War*, 8, 6B, p. 606; see also p. 584.

54 Clausewitz, *Vom Kriege*, 8, 6A, p. 887.

55 Clausewitz, *Strategie aus dem Jahr 1804*, p. 51.

56 Clausewitz, *Principles of War*, p. 38.

57 *On War*, 8, 1, Jolles, p. 567.

58 Ibid., 8, 6A, p. 603; see also 1, 2, p. 91; 2, 5, p. 159; 7, 5, p. 528; 7, 22, p. 570.

59 Ibid., 1, 1, para 7, Jolles, pp. 8–9; Howard and Paret do not use 'absolute' in their translation, although the German demands it.

60 Ibid., 1, 1, p. 87.
61 Ibid., 1, 1, Jolles, p. 16.
62 Ibid., 1, 1, Jolles, p. 10.
63 Ibid., 1, 1, p. 89.
64 Ibid., 6, 21, p. 453; see also 1, 3, p. 100.
65 Clausewitz, 'Die Feldzüge von 1799', p. 547.
66 *On War*, 1, 1, p. 76.
67 Ibid., 1, 1, pp. 86–7; see also 1, 1, p. 76; 1, 1, p. 81; 3, 6, pp. 191–2.
68 Ibid., 3, 17, p. 220.
69 Clausewitz, *Schriften*, edited by Hahlweg, vol. 1, pp. 661–9.
70 *On War*, 3, 17, p. 220.
71 Clausewitz, *Historical and Political Writings*, pp. 318–24.
72 Clausewitz, 'Strategische Übersicht des Feldzugs von 1815', pp. 320–21; see also *On War*, 6, 6, p. 372.
73 Clausewitz, *Strategie aus dem Jahr 1804*, p. 76; *On War*, 3, 4, pp. 186–8; 5, 2, p. 281; 5, 16, p. 347; 5, 17, p. 350; 6, 3, p. 365; 6, 6, p. 372: 6, 21, p. 452; 6, 25, p. 473; 7, 20, p. 563.
74 *On War*, 6, 26, Jolles, p. 457.
75 Ibid., 6, 26, p. 483.
76 Ibid., Howard and Paret, p. 70, translate 'major war' as 'major operations' and 'theory of major war' as 'theory of war', so diminishing the significance of what Clausewitz is saying on this point; see Hahlweg's introduction to Clausewitz, *Schriften*, vol. 1, pp. 38–9.
77 Clausewitz, *Schriften*, edited by Hahlweg, vol. 1, p. 443; the notes embrace pp. 226–588.
78 Ibid., p. 237.
79 Ibid., pp. 429, 443–5.
80 Ibid., p. 239; see also pp. 228–39.

81 Ibid., pp. 380, 394.
82 Ibid., vol. 1, pp. 740–1.
83 *On War*, 6, 26, Jolles, p. 457.
84 Ibid., 6, 26, Howard and Paret, p. 481.

Conclusion

1 *On War*, 6, 28, p. 488.
2 Ibid., 8, 3B, p. 593.
3 Letter to Gneisenau, 17 June 1811, Clausewitz, *Schriften*, edited by Hahlweg, vol. 1, pp. 640–5; see also letter to Gneisenau, 11 April 1824, in ibid., vol. 2, p. 445; *On War*, 5, 4, pp. 285–91.
4 *Vom Kriege*, 1, 1, Hahlweg, p. 111. The English translations of this passage all translate *Natur* as 'character' or 'characteristics'; the German suggests something more essential than superficial.

SOURCES AND FURTHER READING

There is no definitive edition of Clausewitz's writings, a scholarly black hole which has rightly amazed successive generations of commentators. The result is bibliographical confusion. Marie von Brühl and her brother were responsible for *Hinterlassene Werke des Generals Carl von Clausewitz über Krieg und Kriegführung* (Berlin, Dümmler, 1832–7). The first three of the ten volumes embraced *Vom Kriege*, the next five the campaigns of the French Revolutionary and Napoleonic Wars, and the last two wars between 1630 and 1793. Reference to the publishing history of *Vom Kriege*, both in German and English, has been made in the introduction and in chapter 2. In 1999 Wolfgang von Seidlitz edited reprints of volumes 4 to 8 of the *Hinterlassene Werke*, under the title *Sämtliche Schriften 'Vom Kriege'* (Mundus, 1999), with the implication that the remainder were to follow. The French have announced their intention to produce a complete edition of the works, an undertaking aided by the fact that volumes 4 to 8 have already been translated into French and were reprinted between 1972 and 1999 (Paris, Agora, Pocket). The instructions of 1812 written for the Crown Prince, which appeared as an appendix to the original edition of *Vom Kriege*, were published in English by Hans Gatzke as *Principles of War* (London, John Lane, the Bodley Head, 1943). The only one of the military histories to have appeared in English is *The Campaign of 1812 in Russia* (1843; reprint, New York, Da Capo, 1995).

Clausewitz wrote a great deal more than was published in the *Hinterlassene Werke*. However, these writings are scattered, and the vast majority are unavailable in English. The most important for the evolution of Clausewitz's thinking are *Strategie aus dem Jahr 1804 mit Zusätzen von 1808 und 1809* (Hamburg, Hanseatische Verlagsanstalt, 1937), edited by Eberhard Kessel, and *Preussen in seiner grossen Katastrophe*, published by the Grosse Generalstab in 1880 (reprint, Vienna, Karolinger, 2001). The collection translated and edited by Peter Paret and Daniel Moran, *Historical and Political Writings* (Princeton, Princeton University Press, 1992) is revealing, but eschews the principal military works. Again, the French are better served, in this case by Marie-Louise Steinhauser, whose *De la Révolution à la Restauration. Ecrits et Lettres* (Paris, Gallimard, 1976), contains selections from most of the obvious bodies of material, as does the widely available DDR volume, Carl von Clausewitz, *Ausgewählte militärische Schriften*, edited by Gerhard Förster and Dorothea Schmidt (Berlin, Militärverlag der Deutschen Demokratischen Republic, 1981). The product of an earlier ideological enthusiasm for Clausewitz is *Geist und Tat*, edited by Walther Malmsten

Schering (Berlin, Alfred Kröner, 1941), which prints documents which have now been lost, as does Hans Rothfels (ed.), *Politische Schriften und Briefe* (Munich, Drei Masken, 1922). Clausewitz's principal correspondents were his wife, Marie von Brühl, and Gneisenau. The letters to Marie were first published by Karl Schwartz, *Leben des Generals Carl von Clausewitz und der Frau Marie von Clausewitz* (Berlin, Berl, 1878) and have been reprinted in various editions, some more anxious to heighten the romance of a love story played out against the backdrop of the Napoleonic wars than to illuminate military thought. Karl Linnebach's *Karl u. Marie von Clausewitz. Ein Lebensbild in Briefen und Tagebuchblättern* (Berlin, Martin Warneck, 1917) avoids the worst of the pitfalls. The Gneisenau correspondence appears in its entirety, together with the lectures on small war, drafts for *Vom Kriege*, and other pieces, in the most scholarly edition of Clausewitz's writings, *Schriften-Aufsätze-Studien-Briefe* (2 vols in three parts, Göttingen, Vandenhoeck & Ruprecht, 1966–90), edited by Werner Hahlweg. But Hahlweg eschewed much that had already been published and therefore did not produce the definitive edition of Clausewitz's papers which is so badly needed.

English-language readers, poorly served in other respects, can at least read the best biography of Clausewitz in any language: Peter Paret, *Clausewitz and the State* (Oxford, Oxford University Press, 1976). Paret's other writings on Clausewitz have been collected as *Understanding*

War (Princeton, Princeton University Press, 1992). His co-translator, Michael Howard, has produced a typically pithy and brief account of the man and his thought, *Clausewitz* (Oxford, Oxford University Press, 1983). The nearest equivalent in German is Werner Hahlweg, *Clausewitz. Soldat-Politiker-Denker* (Göttingen, Musterschmidt-Verlag, 1969). However, the more important of the German biographies is Hans Rothfels, *Carl von Clausewitz. Politik und Krieg* (Berlin, Dümmler, 1920; reprint, Bonn, 1980), which focuses on the years up to 1815.

Clausewitz's intellectual development and trajectory have attracted philosophers in particular, whose insights should not be neglected by historians just because they can ride rough-shod over their sense of chronology. In German, Walther Malmsten Schering, *Die Kriegsphilosophie von Clausewitz* (Hamburg, Hanseatische Verlagsanstalt, 1935) is more important than its association with the Third Reich allows for. The most significant German works since 1945 have been those by Herfried Münkler, *Über den Krieg. Stationen der Kriegsgeschichte im Spiegel ihrer theoretischen Reflexion* (Weilerswist, Velbrück, 2002), who discusses the advocate of 'existential war' in 1812, and Andreas Herberg-Rothe, *Das Rätsel Clausewitz* (Munich, Wilhelm Fink, 2001), who shows the importance of Clausewitz's historical writings to the composition of *On War*. In English, W. B. Gallie, *Philosophers of Peace and War: Kant, Clausewitz, Marx, Engels and Tolstoy* (Cambridge, Cambridge University Press, 1978) was eclipsed by the other books with which it was contemporary. Of far greater impact was Raymond Aron, *Penser la guerre, Clausewitz* (2 vols, Paris, Gallimard, 1976), mangled in its English translation, *Clausewitz: Philosopher of War* (London, Routledge & Kegan Paul, 1983). Aron's essays were reprinted as *Sur Clausewitz* (Brussels, Editions Complexe, 1987). Both Hervé Guineret, *Clausewitz et la guerre* (Paris, Presses Universitaires de France, 1999) and Emmanuel Terray, *Clausewitz* (Paris, Fayard, 1999) engage with Aron's legacy. On the impact of science on Clausewitz, see Alan Beyerchen, 'Clausewitz, nonlinearity, and the unpredictability of war', *International Security*, 17, 3 (winter 1992–3), pp. 59–90.

Clausewitz's place in the evolution of military thought is the subject of Azar Gat's *The Origins of Military Thought* (Oxford, Oxford University Press, 1989), an important corrective to Paret. It is also explored in the introductions by Hahlweg to his edition of *Vom Kriege* and by Peter Paret and Michael Howard in their translation. It is a theme most recently discussed by Beatrice Heuser in *Reading Clausewitz* (London, Pimlico, 2002). Ulrich Marwedel, *Carl von Clausewitz. Persönlichkeit und Wirkungsgeschichte seines Werkes bis 1918* (Boppard am Rhein, Harald Boldt, 1978), considers the impact of his work until 1918, particularly in Germany, and P. M. Baldwin looks at his use by the Nazis, in 'Clausewitz in Nazi Germany', *Journal of Contemporary History*, 16 (1981), pp. 5–26. Dallas D. Irvine's article, 'The French discovery of Clausewitz and Napoleon', *Journal of the American Military Institute* (vol. 4, no. 3, 1942, pp. 143–61), can be supplemented by works such as Hubert Camon, *Clausewitz* (Paris, R. Chapelot, 1911) and Général Palat [Pierre Lehautcourt], *La philosophie de la guerre d'après Clausewitz* (Paris, Charles-Lavauzelle, 1921; reprinted Economica, 1998). Christopher Bassford, *Clausewitz in English: The reception of Clausewitz in Britain and America 1815–1945* (Oxford, Oxford University Press, 1994), runs beyond its declared end date into the Cold War. But Clausewitz's impact on post-1945 strategy is probably best explored through works like Stephen J. Cimbala, *Clausewitz and Escalation: Classical perspectives on nuclear strategy* (London, Frank Cass, 1991), and collections of essays such as *Freiheit ohne Krieg? Beiträge zur Strategie-Diskussion der Gegenwart im Spiegel der Theorie von Carl von Clausewitz*, edited by Eberhard Wagemann and Joachim Niemeyer for the Clausewitz-Gesellschaft (Bonn, Dümmler, 1980), and Gunther Dill (ed.), *Clausewitz in Perspektive. Materialen zu Carl von Clausewitz: Vom Kriege* (Frankfurt am Main, Ullstein, 1980). In English, Michael I. Handel (ed.), *Clausewitz and Modern Strategy* (London, Frank Cass, 1986) included essays on national responses to Clausewitz in historical perspective. Handel's own book, *Masters of War: Sun Tzu, Clausewitz and Jomini* (London, Frank Cass, 1992), was much expanded by the time it reached its third edition in 2001. Examinations of Clausewitz's thinking published since the end of the Cold War include: Hugh Smith, *On Clausewitz: A study of military and political ideas* (Basingstoke, Palgrave, 2005), which has a textbook quality to it;

Benoît Durieux, *Relire 'De la Guerre' de Clausewitz* (Paris, Economica, 2005), which summarizes the book but also puts it in the context of current defence debates; and David Lonsdale, *The Nature of War in the Information Age: Clausewitzian future* (London, Frank Cass, 2004), which uses Clausewitz to argue that the nature of war is unchanged. Barry D. Watts put the case for friction's continuing importance in *Clausewitzian Friction and Future War* (McNair Paper 52, National Defense University, 1996). As part of this debate, Clausewitz's ideas on small war have gained in currency through T. Derbent, *Clausewitz et la guerre populaire* (Brussels, Aden [2004]), and Lennart Souchon (ed.), 'Kleine Krieg', with articles by Ulrike Kleemeier, Jürgen Frese and Beatrice Heuser, in *Clausewitz-Information 1/2005* (Hamburg, Führungsakademie der Bundeswehr, 2004). Such studies have noted Clausewitz's influence on Lenin, and for his reception in Russia more generally, see Olaf Rose, *Carl von Clausewitz: zur Wirkungsgeschichte seines Werkes in Russland und der Sowjetunion 1836 bis 1991* (Munich, Oldenbourg, 1995).

INDEX

Index compiled by Meg Davies, Fellow of the Society of Indexers

Also available in the *Books that Shook the World* series, by **Manjul Publishing House**

The Bible
The Biography

KAREN ARMSTRONG

The Bible is the most widely distributed book in the world. Translated into over two thousand languages, it is estimated that more than six billion copies have been sold in the last two hundred years alone. In this seminal account Karen Armstrong traces the story of the gestation of the Bible to reveal it as a complex and contradictory document created by scores of people over hundreds of years.

Karen Armstrong tells of the development of both the Hebrew Bible and the New Testament, drawing on the disparate sources that formed these sacred texts. From the Jewish practice of Midrash and the Christian cult of Jesus to the influence of Paul's letters on the Reformation and the manipulation of Revelations by Christian fundamentalists, Armstrong explores the different ways in which these sixty-six books have been understood and identifies the social needs that they answered. In the process she demonstrates the Bible is a fascinatingly unfamiliar and paradoxical work. The result will permanently alter our understanding of this most crucial of books.

'Armstrong's great achievement is that, as well as leaving you with a clearer, more historically accurate picture as to what precisely the Bible is (and isn't), she also makes you want to go back and read it again with fresh eyes.' Peter Stanford, *Independent*

MANJUL
Manjul Publishing House
Religion
978-81-8322-133-7

Also available in the *Books that Shook the World* series, by **Manjul Publishing House**

Darwin's Origin of Species
A Biography

JANET BROWNE

No book has changed people's understanding of themselves more than Darwin's *Origin of Species*. Its publication in 1859 caused a sensation, and it went out to become an international bestseller. The theory of natural selection shocked readers, calling into question the widely held belief that there was a Creator.

Here, Janet Browne, Darwin's foremost biographer, describes with bracing clarity the genesis, reception and legacy of Darwin's theories, and how his work altered forever our knowledge of what it is to be human.

'Superb: easy to read but none the less intellectually exciting... the perfect introduction to Darwin's thought.'
Adam Sisman, *Sunday Telegraph*

'A gem... Browne explains with absolute clarity and readability the sources, nature, reception and legacy of *On the Origin of Species*.'
A. C. Grayling, *The Times*

'Brownie relates the history of Darwin's ideas with a pellucid freshness that makes reading the book a continuous pleasure.'
John Gray, *New Statesman*

MANJUL

Manjul Publishing House
Popular Science
978-81-8322-103-0

Also available in the *Books that Shook the World* series, by **Manjul Publishing House**

Thomas Paine's Rights of Man
A Biography

CHRISTOPHER HITCHENS

Thomas Paine is one of the greatest political advocates in history. His most famous work, *Declaration of the Rights of Man*, is a passionate defence of man's inalienable rights, inspired by his outrage at Edmund Burke's attack on the uprising of the French people.

Since its publication in 1791, *Rights of Man* has been both celebrated and maligned, but here Christopher Hitchens marvels at its forethought and revels in its contentiousness. Above all, Hitchens demonstrates how Paine's book forms the philosophical cornerstone of the first democratic republic.

'A timely book.' Billy Bragg, *Observer* Books of the year

'Christopher Hitchens is at his characteristically incisive best.' A. C. Grayling, *The Times*

'A brilliant portrait of Paine.' Jonathan Ree, *Prospect*

Also available in the *Books that Shook the World* series, by **Manjul Publishing House**

Marx's Das Kapital
A Biography

FRANCIS WHEEN

Das Kapital was born in a two-room flat in Soho. The first volume was published in 1867 to muted praise, but, after Marx's death, went on to influence thinkers, writers and revolutionaries, from George Bernard Shaw to Lenin.

Francis Wheen's brilliant assessment traces the book's history, from Mark's twenty-year fight – amid political squabbles and personal tragedy – to complete his masterpiece, through to the enormous impact it has had on the course of global history. It is the perfect introduction to both the man and his legacy.

'As gripping and as readable as a first-rate thriller.' A. C. Grayling, *The Times*

'Exhilarating... Wheen provides a vivid portrait of the man.' Adam Sisman, *Sunday Telegraph*

'A brilliant account.' Jonathan Derbyshire, *Time Out*

MANJUL

Manjul Publishing House
Politics
978-81-8322-102-3

Forthcoming in the *Books that Shook the World* series,
by **Manjul Publishing House**

Homer's the Iliad and the Odyssey
A Biography

ALBERTO MANGUEL

The stories of the Trojan war and Helen of Troy, Pantroclus and Achilles, the Sirens and the Cyclops are embedded in western culture, yet readers are often aware that they were made famous by two epic poems, the *Iliad* and the *Odyssey*, and one blind poet: Homer.

Starting with their inception in ancient Greece, Homer's the Iliad and the Odyssey shows how these poems have reverberated through the western canon, from the Rome of Virgil and Horace to Joyce's Dublin and Derek Walcott's Caribbean, via Dante and Racine. In this lyrical and graceful book, Alberto Manguel delights in the original poems and celebrates their presence throughout history.

'What Alberto Manguel gives us in his biography of the *Iliad* and the *Odyssey* is nothing less than a history of literature itself.'
Tom Holland, *Spectator*

'A dizzying and... hugely enjoyable tour of the Homeric project, from antiquity to the present day: from Virgil's remaking of the Iliad and the Odyssey into the Roman national epic, to scholars in medieval Baghdad who could recite Homer word for word from memory, and to the dramatic retelling of the Iliad by Alessandro Baricco... A hugely stimulating read.'
Mary Beard, *The Times*

MANJUL

Manjul Publishing House
Classics
978-81-8322-147-4

Forthcoming in the *Books that Shook the World* series,
by **Manjul Publishing House**

On the Wealth of Nations

P. J. O' ROURKE

Adam Smith's *The Wealth of Nations* was first published in 1776 and was almost instantly recognized as fundamental to an understanding of economics. It was also recognized as being really long; and as P. J. O'Rourke points out, to fully understand *The Wealth of Nations*, the cornerstone of free-market thinking and a book that shapes the world to this day, you also need to be familiar with Smith's earlier doorstopper, *The Theory of Moral Sentiments*. But now you don't have to read either, because P. J. has done it for you.

In this brilliant and indispensable book P. J. O'Rourke shows us why Smith is still relevant and why what seems obvious now was once so revolutionary.

'Consistently funny, with cracking asides... O'Rourke is a glittering writer, light but punchy, wry and impassioned, witheringly witty one moment and rambunctiously sarcastic the next... If you're daunted by *The Wealth of Nations*, O'Rourke's riff on it is the next best thing.'
Stuart Kelly, *Scotland on Sunday*

'P.J. O'Rourke has done the hard work for you by taking the 900-page masterpiece and compressing its ideas into a little over 200 breezy pages... His wit can be razor sharp.'
Alex Moffatt, *Irish Times*

'Sophisticated and comprehensive... For those without the stomach to read the real thing, P.J. O'Rourke's book will provide an unusually enjoyable starting point.'
Allister Health, *Literary Review*

MANJUL

Manjul Publishing House
Economics
978-81-8322-153-5